A 90-DAY [

Awakening to God's Kingdom Within

DAILY ENCOURAGEMENT
FOR KINGDOM LIVING

MATT TOMMEY

Contents

Introduction

My friend, I'm so happy you've started this journey to encourage yourself in the Lord. This devotional is based on my best-selling book, *God's Plan for Living*, and gives you practical, daily encouragement for living as you awaken your heart to the Kingdom of God already living within you. Each day, you'll find a faith-building affirmation, scripture verse, devotional, and prayer designed to help you draw closer to the Lord and all He has for you as you pursue God's IDEAL.

Just in case you're not familiar, God's IDEAL is a simple framework for Kingdom living (developed and unpacked in *God's Plan for Living*) that includes the following precepts: Identity, Design, Expansion, Alignment, and Love. Essentially, God's IDEAL teaches that as you establish your identity in Christ, your unique design is uncovered, and your Kingdom assignment is revealed. Then, as you faithfully walk with God, He will be faithful to align and refine your heart, enabling you to walk in the fullness of His love. A simple but powerful roadmap.

Each devotion in this book is designed to help deepen your understanding of these Biblical Kingdom principles and awaken your heart to the powerful, eternal Kingdom of God that lives within every believer in Jesus. As you align your heart and mind with the truths found in God's Word and begin to cultivate them, your life will be transformed.

Thanks again for joining me for the next 90 days. I pray this devotional book will be one you'll revisit again and again to encourage yourself in the Lord and walk into all He has for you.

Many Blessings,

Matt

How to Use This Devotional Book

As we begin our journey together, I encourage you to use this book as a springboard to more extended time with the Lord. Although brief, each daily entry is packed with truth from God's Word. To get the most out of each day, I encourage you to:

Read

Read each entry slowly and listen with the ears of your heart. You may want to take time to look up the scripture verse for the day and read the verses around it to understand the context of the verses more fully.

Meditate

After reading the devotional, take time to meditate on what was shared. Ask the Holy Spirit to awaken your heart to the truth He wants to show you and the ways you can implement the truth that was shared.

Journal

Take your favorite journal and write your response to that day's devotion as well as what the Holy Spirit showed you. Allow this to be a moment of free expression as you pour out your heart to the Lord voicing your thanks, praises, frustrations and requests.

Listen

As you write, listen to God's voice and pay attention to the thoughts, nudges, feelings, pictures and/or impressions you sense Holy Spirit offering during this time. We all see in part on this journey of discovery. Embrace the grace-filled process of learning to perceive the voice of the Holy Spirit as you listen for His clarity and direction rather than being filled with the fear of potential penalty for getting something wrong.

Pray

Pray the prayer at the end as a way to close your time with the Lord and move into the rest of your day.

Day 1

I Am Seen & Known by God

"O LORD, you have examined my heart and know everything about me. You know when I sit down or stand up. You know my thoughts even when I'm far away. You see me when I travel and when I rest at home. You know everything I do. You know what I am going to say even before I say it, LORD. You go before me and follow me. You place your hand of blessing on my head. Such knowledge is too wonderful for me, too great for me to understand!"

Psalm 139:1-6 NLT

Every person desires to be seen and known. To be understood and to connect deeply with others on life's journey. Yet, when life gets busy, it's easy to feel alone in the crowd. Present, but hidden. Seen, but not known. Heard, but not understood.

In those moments, we can take comfort in knowing we are seen and known completely by God. There is nothing hidden from Him, not even our innermost thoughts, dreams and fears. And no matter how we feel, there is nothing that can separate us from His love.

Whether you're going through the normal routine of your day or taking a rest, He sees you. Achieving or failing, He loves you. Whether struggling with the emotions of a difficult situation, He empathizes with you. When you feel like no one around you understands, rest assured He knows you inside and out. And in those moments, whether you feel like it or not, you are blessed.

Prayer

"Father, thank you that you see and know me more deeply than any human ever could. In moments of weakness and times of strength, you have called me blessed. I rest in your love today, knowing that I am not alone. You go before me and behind me. In my rising and sleeping, you are with me. Increase my awareness of you today, I pray in Jesus' name, amen."

Day 2

I Am God's Masterpiece

"For we are God's masterpiece. He has created us anew in Christ Jesus, so we can do the good things he planned for us long ago."

Ephesians 2:10 NLT

When we think of the word masterpiece, images of great historical artworks may come to mind. But that's how our heavenly Father sees you and me right now: as His masterpiece. We may not be used to thinking of ourselves this way, but God does. He sees us: complete, whole, and beautifully unique in Christ. Fully able to reveal and reflect His image to others.

Even still, it's easy to downplay our uniqueness in God's Kingdom when it seems everyone, including Satan, is trying to get us to reject who God created us to be. The original word used for masterpiece comes from the root word, poéma which is where we get the word poem. Think of that! We are designed as a poem. The unique creative expression of God to reveal and release His nature in the world!

When you embrace your unique divine design, you come into agreement with all God has planned for you as His child, including all the grace, favor, and momentum to walk it out. But without embracing your unique design, gifts, and graces, you forfeit God's plans for your life and often operate in comparison, shame, fear, and manipulation. Don't settle for the mundane life of a religious clone.

Prayer

"Father, thank you for creating me as your unique poem to reveal and reflect your image to others in the world. When you made me, you called me very good. And you still do today. Thank you for the incredible life you have planned for me in your Kingdom. Things so good, I can't even begin to imagine what they look like. But I trust you because you're a good Father. You love me, you are with me, and you promise to never leave me. Thank you for creating me uniquely, in Jesus' name, amen."

Day 3

I Am Filled with Hope

"…the mystery which has been hidden from ages and from generations, but now has been revealed to His saints. To them, God willed to make known what are the riches of the glory of this mystery among the Gentiles: which is Christ in you, the hope of glory."

Colossians 1:26-27 NKJV

In moments of desperation, it's easy to lose hope and cry out to God, as if He's somehow distant and removed from the problems of life. Fear can easily set in, causing us to lose faith in God and all that He has done for us through Christ. But be reminded today that as a believer in Jesus, our hope comes from who's on the inside, not what's going on outside.

Through the supernatural mystery of our salvation, Christ lives inside us in all His fullness. Our bodies are the temple of the Holy Spirit. We have been restored to His Kingdom with all its blessings and benefits and given the Holy Spirit to guide us into all wisdom, knowledge, and understanding.

Instead of looking for hope in external things, rest in the that fact Christ is living inside you. As you walk with Him today, intentionally raise your awareness of His presence within. Remember, your confident hope is based on what Jesus has already accomplished on your behalf. And as His image bearer, God wants to use you to reveal that glorious hope to others here on earth.

Prayer

"Father, thank you for the gift of hope I now have because Christ lives in me. Hope for eternity and hope for today. Peace for what is to come and peace in this moment. Let an awareness of your supernatural hope fill me afresh and let me be a conduit of that hope to others. I pray in Jesus' name, amen."

Day 4

I Am a Difference Maker

*"You are the salt of the earth. But what good is salt
if it has lost its flavor? Can you make it salty again?
It will be thrown out and trampled underfoot as
worthless. You are the light of the world—like a
city on a hilltop that cannot be hidden. No one
lights a lamp and then puts it under a basket.
Instead, a lamp is placed on a stand, where it gives
light to everyone in the house."*

Matthew 5:13-15 NLT

Tasting a favorite dish when it's perfectly seasoned is a
wonderful experience. Done well, seasoning makes a
big difference! It accentuates the natural flavor of the
food and brings seemingly disparate ingredients into
culinary harmony. In the same way, we were designed
to bring the flavor of Christ to the world. You and I are
difference-makers!

Without knowing Christ, life can seem blah,
uninspiring, and undesirable. Just like food with no
seasoning or a room with no light. Thankfully, God's

remedy was to design every believer as salt and light. As the flavor and brightness of Christ in us overflow to others, they will see the beauty of God for themselves. Experience what life in the Kingdom is all about. Taste and see that the Lord is good because of His demonstrated goodness in our lives.

When you're tempted to shrink back and hide your unique expression of God's Kingdom, take heart! And remember, you were created to be a light in a dark and unsavory world.

Prayer

"Father, thank you for creating me to make a difference in this world and for my unique Kingdom design that shows forth your love and demonstrates the reality of your Kingdom everywhere I go. Thank you that as I walk in who you made me to be, empowered by your Spirit, lives will be changed. I pray this in Jesus' name, amen."

Day 5

I Have Everything I Need

"His divine power has given us everything we need for a godly life through our knowledge of him who called us by his own glory and goodness. Through these he has given us his very great and precious promises, so that through them you may participate in the divine nature, having escaped the corruption in the world caused by evil desires."

2 Peter 1:3-4 NIV

Years ago, people wrote checks for just about everything. As a young man, I remember being amazed that you could pay someone with a slip of paper rather than having to give them actual money! How could this be? The check alone was not currency, nor did it have any inherent value. It was just a slip of paper.

But here's the secret. What makes a check valuable isn't the paper; it's the promise behind it—that the person who signed the check can be trusted to cover the debt when the check is cashed. In the same way, God has given us everything we need to live, grow and thrive in life. He's written us a check and we can take that check to the bank because God is faithful. He backs his promises with His Word and does what He says He will do. Every time!

As you receive what He's promised by faith, and believe and act upon God's promises, you will be empowered with the supernatural ability to walk in the fullness of the Kingdom. What you need for this life doesn't come through begging God or merely hoping things will change. It comes through your firm belief in the promises of God and your faith-filled steps of obedience.

Prayer

"*Father, thank you for giving me everything I need to live, grow and thrive as a child in your Kingdom. Through your precious promises, I have need of nothing. Thank you, Jesus, for your finished work on the cross that restored me to the fullness of your Kingdom. Lord, I receive by faith, every good thing you have for me today. In Jesus' name I pray, amen.*"

Day 6

I Am Alive in Christ

"When he died, he died once to break the power of sin. But now that he lives, he lives for the glory of God. So you also should consider yourselves to be dead to the power of sin and alive to God through Christ Jesus."

Romans 6:10-11 NLT

When you think about yourself, do you consider yourself just an old sinner, barely saved by God's grace, struggling through this life just to make it? Or do you see yourself as a redeemed child of the living God, alive in Christ, and able to do all things through His strength? What we think about ourselves makes a huge difference.

Jesus' death and resurrection broke the power sin had upon God's children once and for all. Instead of being a slave to guilt, fear, and shame, we have been fully redeemed from sin's penalty and reconciled to a life-giving relationship with the Father. But the transformative power of that reality is only made manifest in us when we believe it for ourselves.

By grace, God redeemed, reconciled, and restored you to the Kingdom. There's nothing you did to deserve or earn it, it's a gift that must be received by faith. Otherwise, the promise lays dormant. Even though your spirit has been made alive in Christ, your flesh will continue to rise up, seeking to rule you by your old sin-nature. Even though it may feel familiar and sometimes more comfortable, it's no longer who you are. As you purposefully declare yourself dead to sin and alive in Christ, your new Kingdom reality will begin to flourish inside you. You are alive in Christ!

Prayer

"Father, I praise you today for the finished work of the cross, breaking sin's power and influence over me once and for all. I declare today, I am alive in Christ Jesus! Holy Spirit, I give you permission to work inside me, to transform my soul as I renew my mind to my new reality. Lord, have your way. Make me more like Jesus. I pray this in Jesus' name, amen."

Day 7

I Can Hear God's Voice

"My sheep listen to my voice; I know them, and they follow me."

John 10:27 NLT

The human voice is one of the most distinctive identifying characteristics of a person. Most of us can identify a loved one or a friend easily by only hearing their voice. How? Because we've spent so much time with them. The rhythm of their speech patterns and the texture of their voice are familiar to us. We don't need anything else to verify their identity. And just by hearing their voice, we are comforted, encouraged, and can receive instruction from them.

The same is true with God. The more time we spend meditating on His Word and worshipping in His presence, the more familiar His voice becomes. As we get to know Him in a deeper way, we can begin to internally sense when He's speaking in a still, small voice: through a prophetic word or when a scripture jumps off the page.

Recognizing God's voice is one of the hallmarks of being His child. It's meant to be a normal part of the Christian journey, available to everyone. And confidently recognizing His voice gives you faith to respond in obedience and brings an overwhelming sense of His presence. Take time today to listen for His voice, then obey. He knows you. He loves you. He wants to speak to you today.

Prayer

"Father, thank you for the ability to hear your voice through the power of the Holy Spirit. Thank you for wanting to speak to me so I can get to know you better. Holy Spirit, awaken my senses to the voice of the Father, today. Open the eyes of my understanding. Use my imagination and every sense you have given me to hear and respond to your voice today. In Jesus' name, I pray, amen."

Day 8

I Can Have the Desires of My Heart

"Delight yourself also in the LORD, And He shall give you the desires of your heart. Commit your way to the LORD, Trust also in Him, And He shall bring it to pass."

Psalm 37:4-5 NKJV

A religious mindset will always resist the blessing and favor of God because it's often based on feelings of fear, scarcity, and false humility. Being able to accept the fact that God delights in blessing His children in ways that are beautiful and even extravagant just doesn't make sense, because they often only see God as a rescuer and judge, not a loving Father who gives good gifts to His children.

But God loves to bless His children with abundant blessings of every kind as they delight themselves in Him. The issue is never about God's heart to bless us but about whether our hearts are fully devoted to Him. He loves to bless those who delight in Him because

He knows we are transformed in His presence. It's where our desires become aligned with His. Where our motives become purified. Where our hearts become softened to His leadership.

There's no limit to how much blessing God will pour out when your heart is completely His.

As you cultivate your relationship with God, pay attention to the desires that arise and ask God to fulfill them. More than likely, the dreams and desires that emerge out of your heart are His dreams and desires for you. As you delight yourself in Him, you'll get to enjoy the benefits and blessings while God uses you to release His love to others.

Prayer

"Father, thank you for your promise that tells me as I delight in you, you will give me the desires of my heart. Thank you that I can rest assured that your plans will be accomplished in and through my life. Let faith arise in my heart today to dream with you. Use my life for your glory as I live the abundant life you promised me. I pray this in Jesus' name, amen."

Day 9

I Can Live at Rest

"So there remains a Sabbath rest for the people of God. For the one who has entered His rest has himself also rested from his works, as God did from His. Therefore let us be diligent to enter that rest, so that no one will fall, through following the same example of disobedience."

Hebrews 4:9-11 NASB

Life outside of the Kingdom of God is marked by striving, painful toil, and surviving by the sweat of our brow. Although common, none of these experiences are God's best for us. They are part of the curse that came because of Adam and Eve's fall. Separated from God by their sin, they were forced to survive on their own. Unfortunately, many Christians live a similar life today. Redeemed, reconciled, and restored, but not at rest.

Striving and sweating are no longer required in God's Kingdom. All the blessings and benefits of God were restored to us through Christ's finished work on the cross. Instead of worrying about where our next meal or opportunity will come from, we can be at rest, knowing we have a good Father who has promised to take care of us in every area.

Pursue God's rest today by laying all the stress and worry of your day at His feet. Relax. Breathe. Trust that He is at work in your life. Commit to and follow His plans for your life. He is leading you every step of the way. There's no need to worry. You can rest.

Prayer

"Father, thank you that I don't have to worry or be anxious or try to figure everything out on my own. Thank you for working all things together for my good because you love me. Help me to faithfully walk out and pursue my unique assignment and be at rest. I trust you, Father. In Jesus' name, amen."

Day 10

I Am Faithful to God's Assignment

"His lord said to him, 'Well done, good and faithful servant; you have been faithful over a few things, I will make you ruler over many things. Enter into the joy of your lord.'"

Matthew 25:23 NJKV

Remember the Parable of the Talents in Matthew 25? Jesus gave talents (up to 15 years wages per talent) to each of the 3 workers in the field based on their history. One man received five, one man two, and another one talent. In the story, the first two men invested their money, doubling the amount. When the master returned, he rewarded them both with more because they had been faithful with the few. Not only more resources, but also, more joy in their assignment.

That's how the Kingdom works. Investing what God has invested in us is a foundational principle for all believers who want to grow in the Lord. When we walk in the revelation and resources we have been given, it demonstrates to God we can be entrusted with more. And there's no limit to what He will entrust to those whose hearts are completely His.

If you are frustrated, or experiencing a lack of momentum in your life, check if you are being a good steward of God's gifts. Are you faithfully using the tools God has given you to walk in His blessing? When you do, you will experience the joy, momentum. and abundant life Jesus promised you.

Prayer

"Father, thank you for investing supernatural gifts and graces in me for your glory. Thank you for the ideas, opportunities, resources, and relationships you bring my way each day. Holy Spirit, I ask for your wisdom in how to best invest all the Father has given me. I rest in knowing you will bring the acceleration and increase at the right time. Thank you, Father. In Jesus' name I pray, amen."

Day 11

I Can Call Upon the Lord

"The Lord is close to all who call on him, yes, to all who call on him in truth. He grants the desires of those who fear him; he hears their cries for help and rescues them."

Psalm 145:18-19 NLT

In times of trouble, it's natural to call a trusted friend or family member for help. Sometimes we need a solution to a problem or to be rescued from a difficult circumstance. Other times, it's simply a desire to be heard and understood when we're feeling overwhelmed by the issues of life. But no matter how good friends and family are in times like these, no one is better at empathizing with our struggles than our heavenly Father.

God's Word promises that when we call upon Him, regardless of the situation, He hears and will draw near. He's the friend that sticks closer than a brother. The valiant warrior who protects and defends us. He rescues us from the snare of the enemy and sets us high upon a rock out of the enemy's reach.

No matter what you may feel in times of difficulty, as God's child, you are not alone. Call upon the Lord, no matter the situation. He will be faithful to answer you. Rest in His loving arms. He's a good Father who longs to grant the desires of your heart and give you favor as you walk with Him.

Prayer

"Father, thank you for your promise to draw close to me when I call upon your name. You are my faithful Father. In you, I am safe, whole, and secure. Thank you for comforting me when I am hurting and giving me your strength to face the day as I lean into you. Thank you for your presence that surrounds and protects me day by day. In all things, I trust you are leading me in paths of righteousness for your glory. In Jesus' name I pray, amen."

Day 12

I Can Know God's Plan
for My Life

"That is what the Scriptures mean when they say,
"No eye has seen, no ear has heard, and no mind
has imagined what God has prepared for those
who love him." But it was to us that God revealed
these things by his Spirit. For his Spirit searches
out everything and shows us God's deep secrets.
No one can know a person's thoughts except that
person's own spirit, and no one can know God's
thoughts except God's own Spirit. And we have
received God's Spirit (not the world's spirit), so
we can know the wonderful things God has freely
given us."

1 Corinthians 2:9-12 NLT

It's easy to lose faith in God's plans for us amid all the
distractions of life. Old mindsets creep in, unhealthy
habits reappear, and before we know it, we no longer
feel in touch with God's best for our lives. In those
times, it's easy to doubt God's heart and whether He

even has a plan for us, much less believe he wants to reveal it.

Thankfully, God's Word is crystal clear regarding His plans for us. Plans so good we can't even begin to imagine all they entail. Through the revelation of His precious Holy Spirit, which lives inside each of His children, we can clearly know and pursue the things God has for us.

You have not been left alone to fend for yourself. You are endowed with all the blessings and benefits that come with His Kingdom. Ask the Holy Spirit to reveal to you the Father's plans, then begin pursuing them by faith as He leads you.

Prayer

"Father, thank you for the good plans you have for my life, I can't even begin to imagine how wonderful they are with my natural mind. I trust your heart and ask you to reveal these plans and purposes to me through the power of the Holy Spirit. Awaken my spirit to receive every good thing you have for me today. I pray this in Jesus' name, amen."

Day 13

I Am an Overcomer

"You are of God, little children, and have overcome them, because He who is in you is greater than he who is in the world."

I John 4:4 NKJV

The enemy is always looking for people or situations he can use to frustrate, confuse, and destroy the lives of believers and keep us from God's best. And when he does, the mirage he paints can often seem overwhelming. Whether they be family or friends, work colleagues, or just acquaintances in life—unhealthy people with destructive patterns of living often try to take advantage of situations to make themselves look better.

Thankfully, God's Word is clear. No matter how strong the adversary may appear, Christ, once and for all, defeated the powers of the enemy on our behalf. When He died upon the cross and rose on the third day—He made us complete, whole and one with Him. Now, the same power that raised Him from the dead lives in us, His children. Christ lives in you and me!

Because Christ fights on our behalf, we have already won! With Him, we are more than able to face any foe, knowing we are victorious.

Are you facing a battle today that appears overwhelming? Take heart, beloved. You have already overcome through Christ! The One who lives in you is greater than the one who is seeking your defeat.

Prayer

"Father, thank you that as your beloved child, we are in union through Christ. The same power that raised Christ from the dead lives in me. Thank you for making me an overcomer that can face any foe that comes my way, all because you live in me and I am in you. I choose to set my eyes on you today and believe your Word. I declare the enemy is defeated. I proclaim victory over my life in the mighty name of Jesus. Amen!"

Day 14

I Am Not Lacking Anything

"Taste and see that the LORD is good. Oh, the joys of those who take refuge in him! Fear the LORD, you his godly people, for those who fear him will have all they need. Even strong young lions sometimes go hungry, but those who trust in the LORD will lack no good thing."

Psalm 34:7-9 NLT

When the proverbial storms of life begin to blow, we can either try to endure them in our own strength or seek refuge in the Lord. Thankfully, when we need to hide ourselves under the shadow and protection of His wings, there is joy and provision.

The world often sees hiding until a storm or situation passes as weakness. But what seems right to the world rarely aligns with God's Kingdom. When we hide in God's protective shelter, He renews our strength, provides us with joy, and meets all our needs in abundance. When we feel weak, God's strength is made perfect within us, a benefit of living life in the Kingdom as His child.

In the world, it's common for the strong and self-sufficient to go through times of hunger and need. But not so in the Kingdom of God! When you choose to trust the Lord in both good and challenging times, you get the benefit of His comfort, joy, and abundant provision.

Prayer

"Father, thank you for inviting me to run to you when I face the challenges of life. I declare you are my refuge, protector, and provider. In you, I lack nothing. In your presence, I have everything I need to thrive in all you have called me to. No matter what is going on around me, your presence is more than enough to keep and prosper me. Thank you for the promise of your presence, protection, and provision, in Jesus' name, amen."

Day 15

I Can Walk by Faith

"For we walk by faith, not by sight."

2 Corinthians 5:7 NKJV

Growing up, most people are taught to evaluate their circumstances based on what they see and interpret with their natural senses. Admonitions encouraging children to look both ways before crossing the road or not touch a hot stovetop have echoed throughout homes all over the world for as long as there have been children and parents. But when you become a believer in Jesus, it's easy to forget that there's a new way to see and interpret life. One that requires believing, not just seeing.

Life in the Kingdom requires walking by faith, not living according to what we see in the natural. Practical wisdom is valuable, but it doesn't compare to the wisdom and leadership that comes from the Holy Spirit. As we grow in the Lord, our walk with Him will include many opportunities to step out in faith.

Opportunities that make no sense to our natural minds or experience, yet resonate deep in our hearts.

As you take steps of faith under the leadership of the Holy Spirit, you'll see God's confirming hand at work, refining and aligning you with His Kingdom plan. Your heavenly Father can be trusted, even when He leads you to take steps of faith that don't appear to make sense. He's a good Father and has your best interest at heart. Walk boldly with Him!

Prayer

"Father, thank you that when the road before me seems uncertain, I can step out in faith boldly, knowing you are leading my every step. I confess, at times, I've been afraid to step out in faith because things didn't make sense to my natural mind. Help me to grow in confidence as your child so I can boldly step into everything you have for me in your Kingdom. I declare you to be my good Father, and I will follow where you lead. In Jesus' name, I pray, amen."

Day 16

I Will Seek First the Kingdom of God

"Therefore do not worry, saying, 'What shall we eat?' or 'What shall we drink?' or 'What shall we wear?' For after all these things the Gentiles seek. For your heavenly Father knows that you need all these things. But seek first the kingdom of God and His righteousness, and all these things shall be added to you."

Matthew 6:31-33 NKJV

When sin separated humanity from our relationship with the Father, life apart from God's Kingdom became filled with worry and striving. Cursed, man was sentenced to survive through hard work and the sweat of his brow. Thankfully, because of the finished work of Jesus, you and I have been restored to a Kingdom relationship. Set free from the curse, we no longer strive to survive. But it takes an intentional mindset shift to walk in Kingdom life.

In the Kingdom, we receive everything by faith because God has restored it to us by His grace. Every idea, opportunity, resource, and relationship needed to fulfill our God-given design and accomplish our Kingdom assignment has been provided in abundance. There's no need to worry any longer.

Release those old mindsets: worry, fear, and striving. Hand them over to Him. Believe God's promise is true—He will provide in abundance everything you need. In fact, it is available to you today! As you believe, your faith will grow, and He will show you how to receive all he has promised.

Prayer

"Father, thank you for your promised provision based on your goodness and my position as your child, not my performance or striving. Thank you that I no longer have to worry about how my needs are going to be met, how I'm going to accomplish my assignment, or whether I will be able to enjoy life with you. I declare you my sole provider and trust you to show me how to receive the abundant provision you have promised me. In Jesus' name, I pray, amen."

Day 17

I Am a Friend of God

"You are my friends if you do what I command you. I no longer call you servants, because a servant does not know his master's business. Instead, I have called you friends, for everything that I learned from my Father I have made known to you."

Matthew 15:14-15 NIV

Well-meaning religious people often identify more with being servants of God, rather than friends. This mentality is often focused on working for God rather than developing a close relationship with Him that's led by the Spirit. When we define ourselves by our old identities, sinners in need of a savior, rather than restored sons of God, we serve God out of obligation and with false humility.

Friends share a history and a back story. They are intimately involved in each other's lives and trust one another. Friends love—not out of obligation, but out of a deep, genuine care and concern. Jesus boldly declares us His friends, sharing relationship with us and all the Father has given Him.

This is why friends of Jesus obey what He commands. They can trust His heart. They've been through the fire together and have come out on the other side. Are you a true friend of Jesus? When our heart is consumed with love for Him, we will be willing to do whatever He says. That's a true friend of Jesus.

Prayer

"Jesus, thank you for calling me, friend. Thank you for walking with me each day. You know my weaknesses and my strengths. You understand my frailty and my fears. Yet you still choose to call me your friend. Remind me I don't have to perform for you, only trust you. Awaken my heart today to new realms of intimacy with you through your Holy Spirit so I can walk in the fullness of all I was created for. In your name I pray, amen."

Day 18

I Was Made by God

"I will give thanks to You, for I am fearfully and wonderfully made; wonderful are Your works, and my soul knows it very well. My frame was not hidden from You, when I was made in secret, and skillfully wrought in the depths of the earth; your eyes have seen my unformed substance; and in Your book were all written the days that were ordained for me, when as yet there was not one of them."

Psalm 139:14-16 NASB

It's tempting to think there isn't anything that special about us when there are billions of people in the world. A world that judges everyone by achievement and speed. It isn't enough anymore to just be a normal person living a normal life.

But we are not just a blip on the screen of history. An insignificant grain of sand on the shore of time. No! God uniquely formed us—on purpose—for this specific time and place in history. And all the days of our lives have been recorded in God's book. Ordained and established before we ever took a breath.

No matter what you've been through or what you've believed before today, you were created for His purposes. He wants to use your unique design to reveal and reflect His glory while you enjoy the abundant life Jesus promised you in the Kingdom. What a promise!

Prayer

"Father, thank you for my unique design specifically created for your purposes here on earth and for all eternity. Thank you for all the intricacies of your plans for me. Even though I don't understand everything in my past, and my future is unknown, I choose to trust you and your plans for my life. I pray this, in Jesus' name, amen."

Day 19

I Am a Light

"For you were once darkness, but now you are light in the Lord. Live as children of light (for the fruit of the light consists in all goodness, righteousness, and truth)."

Ephesians 5:8-9 NIV

Our external life reflects and reveals who we really are on the inside. Others learn who we are by watching what we do and how we act. Before we believed in Christ, we lived in sin and exhibited the fruit of sin and a heart that sought its own way. A life that demonstrated on the outside the desperation we experienced on the inside. A life apart from Christ.

Now that Christ lives in us and we have been redeemed, reconciled, and restored, our lives can show forth His glory and His light. We can reflect His glory, not our desperation. Think of the great privilege—to be God's light in the world! An ambassador of His truth, beauty, and goodness. A conduit of His love to others so that they too might come to know the restorative power of Christ. Reconciled to offer reconciliation. Forgiven to extend forgiveness. Given undeserved mercy in order to pour undeserved mercy upon others.

As you walk with Christ and are led by the Holy Spirit, attune yourself to His voice. Watch expectantly for opportunities to be His Ambassador of Light. Allow God to use you to touch others and draw them to Himself through the light that you reveal.

Prayer

"Father, thank you for using my life to reveal and release your light and life to others. Help me today, Holy Spirit, to expectantly watch for opportunities to be a conduit of your love and offer mercy to others. Give me eyes to see and ears to hear what you are saying so I can walk in your transforming power and authority. Thank you for the privilege of carrying your light. In Jesus' name, I pray, amen."

Day 20

I Am Guided by God

*"Trust in the LORD with all your heart; do not
depend on your own understanding. Seek his will
in all you do, and he will show you which path
to take."*

Proverbs 3:5-6 NLT

It's easy to respond to life based on our own understanding. Not because we don't want to know what
God thinks but because it's a learned, established habit.
Before coming to know Christ, our own understanding
was the primary mechanism we relied on. Formed over
many years of observation, comparison, feelings, and
opinions, this "normal" way of thinking has led us
through all our life experiences. But there's so much
more.

In God's Kingdom, we can experience a new
normal. How? By inviting the Holy Spirit into our
decision-making process. As we learn to trust God
with our whole heart and go to Him first, rather than
our own opinions or experiences, His voice becomes

louder. His presence becomes stronger. His leadership becomes more familiar. And over time, intentionally relying on God's leadership becomes our new normal.

When we lean on our own understanding, we experience the results of natural wisdom and learned experience. But when we trust in God, we gain the benefit of His Spirit-birthed supernatural solutions and the results they bring. Lean on and trust in Him each day, He will be faithful to lead and guide you.

Prayer

"Father, thank you for your promise to lead and guide me as I trust in you with all my heart. In areas of my life where I've not trusted you fully, I repent. Forgive me, Lord, for forgetting you are my good Father who desires to lead me into all the good things in your Kingdom. Awaken my heart today to your presence so I can fully trust you, in Jesus' name, amen."

Day 21

I Am Filled with Wisdom & Revelation

"...that the God of our Lord Jesus Christ, the Father of glory, may give to you the spirit of wisdom and revelation in the knowledge of Him, the eyes of your understanding being enlightened; that you may know what is the hope of His calling, what are the riches of the glory of His inheritance in the saints, and what is the exceeding greatness of His power toward us who believe, according to the working of His mighty power..."

Ephesians 1:17-19 NKJV

We can perceive many incredible things through our physical eyes and ears. The beauty of a sunrise or the sound of birds chirping on a beautiful spring morning. A babbling brook and the wind blowing gently through the trees in the forest. But as wonderful as these God-given senses are, they're not sufficient to fully grasp the great glory, beauty and goodness of our God. There's no way to understand the vast expanse and depths of His love through our natural senses. It only happens through the power of the Holy Spirit within us.

To understand and experience the immensity of God's love requires a supernatural enlargement of our internal capacity. Most people think they understand love, until they have their first child and something supernatural happens. Their capacity to love and be loved gets exponentially enlarged in a way they never knew was possible.

When you begin to grasp the great love God has for you, it will fundamentally change the way you see, understand, and live in the world.

Prayer

"Father, thank you for your immense love. I pray today, through the power of your Holy Spirit, you will supernaturally enlarge my capacity to experience and understand your love for me, the call on my life, and all you've promised me in your Kingdom. Transform my heart through the power of your love so I can release your great love to others. I pray this in faith, believing, in Jesus' name, amen."

Day 22

I Am Taught by the Holy Spirit

"But the Helper (Comforter, Advocate, Intercessor—Counselor, Strengthener, Standby), the Holy Spirit, whom the Father will send in My name [in My place, to represent Me and act on My behalf], He will teach you all things. And He will help you remember everything that I have told you."

John 14:26 AMPC

Imagine the confusion the disciples must have felt as Jesus told them He was going away. For three years, they had walked with Him. They saw all the miracles Jesus performed and the countless lives that were changed. They listened as Jesus revealed the secrets of the Kingdom to them and the crowds that followed Him. Watched in awe as Jesus stood up to the religious leaders of the day, proclaiming the freedom and liberty available in the Kingdom. And yet, after all this, Jesus was leaving them? What were they to do?

In a world that seems foreign to our life in Christ, we can often feel alone or inadequate when facing the challenges of daily life. And yet, Jesus' promise to the disciples back then is the same for us today. The Father has sent the Holy Spirit to live inside you and me—24/7. Our body is His temple.

As you attune your heart to respond to the Holy Spirit, He will teach you how to live, love, and respond to every life situation. As you ask and respond to His leading, He will awaken your heart to the reality of God's love for you, make you into a vessel of love to others, and remind you of all that Jesus has promised you.

Prayer

"Father, thank you that you have not left me to fend for myself. Thank you for the Holy Spirit who lives in me and is my teacher, guide, comforter, and friend. Holy Spirit, awaken my heart today to your presence. Enable me to hear and respond to your voice in faith I pray, in Jesus' name, amen."

Day 23

I Am Transformed through Renewing My Mind

"Don't copy the behavior and customs of this world, but let God transform you into a new person by changing the way you think. Then you will learn to know God's will for you, which is good and pleasing and perfect."

Romans 12:2 NLT

Every child learns to live life through modeling others and through personal experience. They see the loving smile of their mother and mirror that back to her. They hear the words of their father and try to repeat them, eventually learning language and communication. They feel love and care from those around them, giving them a sense of security and belonging.

Unfortunately, many people have the opposite experience, leading to opposite results. Instead of feeling safe and secure, they develop negative coping mechanisms which reinforce unhealthy thoughts and over time, their life looks nothing like God's best design. They operate from a broken framework. Jesus' finished work on the cross changed all that for you and me. Instead of living life according to a broken internal framework, we can renew our minds according to the truth of God's Word. As we do, our brain fundamentally shifts how we see and experience the world around us.

As you intentionally pursue the renewing of your mind, Holy Spirit will release His power within you, transforming your beliefs, habits, and actions. Although this is a supernatural process, it's something the Holy Spirit does with you, not to you.

Prayer

"Father, thank you that my life can be fundamentally transformed in every area as I cooperate with the Holy Spirit and renew my mind according to your Word. Show me where I have believed the lies of the enemy and relied on my own experience rather than the truth of your Word. Lead me into the freedom of Kingdom living as I am led by the Holy Spirit each day. I pray this in Jesus' name, amen."

Day 24

I Am Living by the Spirit of God

"So he said to me, "This is the word of the LORD to Zerubbabel: 'Not by might nor by power, but by my Spirit,' says the LORD Almighty."

Zechariah 4:6 NIV

Self-sufficiency is often celebrated in Western culture as the primary method for achieving success. From a young age, well-meaning adults teach children proverbs, like, "Work hard and good things will come to you" and "God helps those who help themselves." These become engrained in our subconscious and become our operating system for life as we grow older. While there's nothing inherently wrong with hard work, it's not the sole solution God designed for successful living in His Kingdom.

Ideal life in the Kingdom is based on our relationship with God, not our work for Him. The impact and influence of our lives should be the result of God's power working through us, not our best intentions. No matter how much we do the things we think will please and honor God, none of it matters unless it's birthed in the secret place with Him. We won't experience any supernatural grace or have any eternal impact apart from the power of the Holy Spirit and the presence of God working in and through us.

God has not asked you to rely on your own wealth, power, and resources to make a difference in the world. He's asked you to trust Him fully and cooperate with the Holy Spirit, day by day, in alignment with your design and assignment. As you do, the resources you need will be entrusted to you. They will increase as you invest and steward them well. Trust Him.

Prayer

"Father, thank you that as your child, I can be led and empowered by your Holy Spirit every day of my life. Thank you that I don't have to perform to bring you glory but that I can simply cooperate with you in alignment with my design. Awaken my heart and mind to the power of your Spirit within me. Lead me today, I pray in Jesus' name, amen."

Day 25

I Can Receive Wisdom from God

*"If any of you lacks wisdom, let him ask of God,
who gives to all liberally and without reproach,
and it will be given to him. But let him ask in
faith, with no doubting, for he who doubts is like
a wave of the sea driven and tossed by the wind.
For let not that man suppose that he will receive
anything from the Lord; he is a double-minded
man, unstable in all his ways."*

James 1:5-8 NKJV

Every day, we need wisdom to navigate overwhelming
situations such as financial challenges, relational
conflicts, or work-related circumstances. The enemy
uses these to turn up the pressure and make our lives
seem hopeless. Thankfully, as children of God, we
don't have to face any situation alone. We can ask God
for His wisdom and He promises to give it to us—in
abundance, without blaming us for being unable to
figure it out for ourselves. But there's one condition:
faith.

When we ask God for something in faith, we come into agreement with His powerful promise to give us everything we need in this life, including wisdom. We align ourselves with what God has already done on our behalf and position ourselves to receive. But when we doubt, we are unable to receive what God has for us. Instead, we are tossed to and fro like a little boat on the open sea.

If you want wisdom from God, ask in faith. Declare His willingness and ability to supernaturally provide it for you (based on the scripture above), then expectantly look for His answer. When you do, you will open the unlimited flow of God's wisdom for your life.

Prayer

"Father, thank you for the promise of your super-natural wisdom. Teach me to ask in faith, Holy Spirit, reminding me of the Father's willingness and ability to give me everything I need for this life. Thank you for your faithfulness to me in Jesus' name, amen."

Day 26

I Can Do All Things Through Christ

"Not that I speak in regard to need, for I have learned in whatever state I am, to be content: I know how to be abased, and I know how to abound. Everywhere and in all things I have learned both to be full and to be hungry, both to abound and to suffer need. I can do all things through Christ who strengthens me."

Philippians 4:11-13 NKJV

Life is often filled with situations we would rather avoid. Some are just the problems and troubles of normal life that Jesus promised we would encounter. Sometimes it's the attack of the enemy. Others are opportunities for refinement God brings along to help us grow and mature into the likeness of Christ. Either way, we will face situations that are less than desirable. In those times, how are we to respond?

The godly response to every good, bad, desirable, or undesirable situation is to lean on God's strength rather than our own. As we intentionally cultivate our dependence on the Holy Spirit, our security will shift from circumstantial to being firmly grounded in the power of God. Our identity that was once based on the opinions of others and our own accomplishments becomes rooted in the love of God.

When you receive life and love from God, you can persevere in all circumstances—good or bad. Your ability to endure hardship and/or walk in victory is not based on your strength but God's Spirit working through you. Cultivate that reality in your life and lean upon Him for the strength you need.

Prayer

"Father, thank you that through times of both difficulty and ease, your promise to never leave me or forsake me is sure. Thank you, Holy Spirit, that as I lean upon you, you provide me with the supernatural strength and wisdom I need to live this life. Awaken my heart today to the reality of your power inside of me. I pray this in Jesus' name, amen."

Day 27

I Have Supernatural-Inspired Vision

"When people do not accept divine guidance, they run wild. But whoever obeys the law is joyful."

Proverbs 29:18 NLT

Most people live their lives in reaction mode, responding to life and people moment by moment with no thought of God's calling. Every day, a new priority. Every moment, a new emergency. Over time, this kind of living can wear a person down. A sense of being overwhelmed sets in, along with feelings of discouragement and desperation. The result? They are left to wonder if there's really any purpose to life beyond the day-to-day grind.

Without understanding God's vision for our lives and receiving His divine guidance moment by moment, our tendency will be to bounce around from emergency to emergency and opportunity to opportunity just trying to survive. To try and make something happen on our own. A life of unfulfilled striving and comparison is not God's best plan for our lives. God created us to live life from a place of Spirit-inspired vision: empowered and led by the Holy Spirit.

When you get a clear picture of what God has uniquely called you to do, it gives you the framework for creating priorities that align with His ideal. You can then say yes to things that move you closer to His vision for your life. When you operate from His power, you don't have to make things happen—you can trust He will bring His plans and purposes to fruition through you.

Prayer

"Father, I'm grateful you desire to lead, inspire, and empower me through your Holy Spirit. Thank you for helping me recognize your voice and follow your lead as I pursue my Kingdom assignment. Awaken my heart to see your hand at work in my life today so I can respond in faith. In Jesus' name, I pray, amen."

Day 28

I Am a New Creation in Christ

"Therefore, if anyone is in Christ, he is a new creation; old things have passed away; behold, all things have become new."

2 Corinthians 5:17 NKJV

It's easy to view life through the lens of all the difficult things you've been through. Feeling defined by our mistakes and patterns of sin, one of the most effective strategies of the enemy, creates an overwhelming sense of inadequacy inside our hearts that's almost impossible to shake off. Viewing life's opportunities through our limitations creates an internal turmoil that can make living the Christian life seem impossible and causes many to give up and settle for much less than Jesus promised.

Thankfully, God never intended for us to live life in His Kingdom in our own strength. His plan, from the very beginning, was that we live connected to and empowered by His Spirit. Our old nature has been put to death. Our spirit has been redeemed, reconciled, and restored to the Father's original intent. Through the power of the Holy Spirit, the risen Christ enables us to see and do all things without human limitation.

Each day, you have a choice to cultivate this new reality in Christ or to live life like you did before you were made new. Today, you are a new creation in Christ. Living life from that reality brings you untold possibilities. Choose to amplify your new identity in Christ by setting your heart and mind on this truth. As you do, your internal framework will begin to shift into alignment with the truth of God's Word, forever transforming you from the inside out.

Prayer

"Thank you, Father, for making me a new creation in Christ. Thank you for putting my old sin-nature to death once and for all. I am no longer a slave to sin and its consequences. I can now view life through your perspective and live my life through your strength. Empower me today, Holy Spirit, to walk in this new reality. In Jesus' name, amen."

Day 29

I Am a Child of God

"But as many as received Him, to them He gave the right to become children of God, to those who believe in His name: who were born, not of blood, nor of the will of the flesh, nor of the will of man, but of God."

John1:12-13 NKJV

Nobody has a perfect family experience. Thinking of family can bring up all sorts of emotions. For some, it may evoke happy memories of special times gone by—like birthday parties and Christmas mornings opening gifts together in your pajamas. For others, it may be a reminder of difficult times, stirring painful emotions. Even though the family was originally designed by God to give us a picture of what life lived through love and connection should look like, everyone has experienced dysfunctional family dynamics.

Thankfully, in Christ, we've been brought into a new, healthy family: the family of God.

You have been adopted as God's child through the finished work of Jesus. You did nothing to earn it. This gift was God's intention from the beginning of time. The Father wants to redeem and restore your view of what a real family was designed to be, a place of safety and comfort, acceptance and belonging. You are no longer an orphan trying to survive on your own. You are accepted, loved, and provided for because of His grace.

Prayer

"Father, thank you for making me your child through the finished work of Jesus. Thank you for placing me into your eternal family where I am fully accepted and completely loved. Thank you for seeing me, knowing me and yet still desiring to be in deep relationship with me. And that as your child, I have everything I need and am no longer alone. I pray this, in Jesus' name, amen."

Day 30

I Am Secure in God's Love for Me

"Though I walk in the midst of trouble, you preserve my life; you stretch out your hand against the wrath of my enemies, and your right hand delivers me. The LORD will fulfill his purpose for me; your steadfast love, O LORD, endures forever. Do not forsake the work of your hands."

Psalm 138:7-8 ESV

Life without an awareness of God's faithfulness can be difficult and overwhelming. When the enemy speaks his lies, our old nature's automatic reflex will always be fear. Everything is seen as impending doom or a hopeless situation. Our natural mind seeks to protect us from harm by convincing us to shrink back, hide and become invisible. But thankfully, in Christ, that doesn't have to be our response.

David knew the reality of living in the shadow of God's wings. In that place, he found safety and an abundance of provision and strength. It is there, under God's wing, His purpose for our lives is often revealed.

No matter how dark the situation may seem, God's power is more than enough to deliver and establish His plans for us. His desire is never for us to shrink back in fear but to be empowered and encouraged in Him.

In moments of difficulty, remember God is faithful to establish His plans in your life as you walk with Him, no matter how hopeless your current situation may seem. Your life on this earth is not by chance. You are God's child and an integral part of His Kingdom story.

Prayer

"Father, thank you for having a wonderful plan for my life in your Kingdom. I declare my trust in you today. You are my good father, my protector, and the preserver of my life. You prepare the way before me and order my steps. Awaken my heart today, Holy Spirit, to hear your voice and respond in faith to the plans you have for me. In Jesus' name, I pray, amen."

Day 31

I Am Fruitful in Christ

"I am the vine, you are the branches. He who abides in Me, and I in him, bears much fruit; for without Me you can do nothing."

John 15:5 NKJV

Life can often feel like a race to a finish line that's always moving. As soon as you're making progress, the destination moves. Over time, this frustration leads to feeling paralyzed or striving. Paralyzed because you feel you're not equal to the task. Striving because you feel you must make something happen on your own to see results. Apart from the life-giving presence of God, it's easy to get worn out.

Thankfully, living in God's Kingdom is wholly different. It's not based on our ability to make things happen on our own. We're not judged by our inability to perform. No! Life in the Kingdom as God's child is based on our ability to receive. As Jesus beautifully described in John 15:5, He is our source – a large, healthy vine that provides life to the branches. As we stay connected to Him, to the vine, all the nutrients and provision we need to thrive and prosper come from Him.

Apart from that life-giving connection, you won't see the fruit you so deeply desire. As a branch, all you must do is stay connected to the vine. In that place of constant connection with Him, your life will bear lasting fruit. As you increase your awareness of His presence today, know He is faithful to provide all you need.

Prayer

"Father, thank you that you are the vine of my life which feeds and nourishes me in every area. I am thankful I don't have to make anything happen or perform for you to receive what I need. You are my good Father. Faithful in all you do. As I remain in you and you remain in me, I will bear much fruit and experience the abundant life you created me for in your Kingdom. I pray this, in Jesus' name, amen."

Day 32

I Can Know Things to Come

*"Behold, the former things have come to pass, and
new things I declare; Before they spring forth I tell
you of them."*

Isaiah 42:9 NKJV

When thinking of living by faith, a picture may come
to mind of someone blindly walking about in the dark.
Trusting God even though they don't understand where
they're going or what their next step in life may be.
There certainly are seasons of life where that is the case,
and it can be quite disconcerting. Everyone likes to
know where they are going and what to expect. That's
normal. Thankfully, God uses these times to teach us to
trust Him more than what we can see.

As restored children of God, we have the promise
of His voice and can respond to His leadership as a
normal part of life. That's not presumptuous or
prideful. It's how life in the Kingdom was designed to
be lived. Just like Adam and Eve, we can walk in the
cool of the day with our Father. Learning to hear and

respond to His voice builds faith. It's walking in the dark with complete trust.

God has declared in the verse above that He will indeed tell you of the new things He has for you. What an exciting promise! When you can't see what's ahead, build up your confidence by remembering that He is willing and able to lead you. Today, ask Him to speak to you about the new things He has planned for you. In the knowing and in the trusting, He will be faithful.

Prayer

"Father, I'm so thankful you desire to speak to me about the issues of life. Thank you for your promise to lead and guide me through every situation, good or challenging. Please show me today the new things I don't yet see and understand. Give me vision, Father, for what's to come so I can come into agreement with your plans and purpose for my life. I pray this, in Jesus' name, amen."

Day 33

I Have a Hope and a Future

"For I know the plans I have for you," declares the LORD, "plans to prosper you and not to harm you, plans to give you hope and a future."

Jeremiah 29:11 NIV

No matter how long we have been walking with the Lord, sometimes we just need a reminder of His goodness and grace, His mercy and power, His plans and purposes for us. The seasons and situations of life can cloud our vision. Our own humanness can magnify our experiences and cause us to fear rather than trust God. Thankfully, as we intentionally turn our hearts to the Lord, listening for His voice, He speaks words of encouragement into our hearts. He reminds us He is not trying to harm but help. In those moments, a shift happens, and our purpose realigns with His.

Seeing life from God's perspective changes everything. Instead of viewing life through the wounded lens of past disappointments and an anxious future, we can expect good things will come. The one who is leading us by His voice will abundantly provide for our every need and protect us by His strong right hand.

Even though you might not understand all the ways your life will unfold, you can trust the one who is walking with you. If you need a new perspective or gentle reminder from the Lord, just ask Him. He's a good father and promises to withhold no good thing from those who walk with Him (Psalm 81:11).

Prayer

"Father, thank you that even when I can't see, feel, or understand your plans for my life, you are faithful. I can trust you because you are my good father. Thank you for reminding me that you aren't trying to harm me but to bring me into all the promise and purpose for which I was designed. Help me to shift my perspective today toward the reality of your Kingdom. In Jesus' name I pray, amen."

Day 34

I Can Fully Love Others

"If someone says, "I love God," and hates his brother, he is a liar; for he who does not love his brother whom he has seen, how can he love God whom he has not seen? And this commandment we have from Him: that he who loves God must love his brother also."

1 John 4:20-21 NKJV

Nobody ever said loving others would be easy. In fact, it's one of the most difficult challenges you'll face as a believer. Jesus was clear that we should love God with our whole being and then, from that love, love others (Mark 12:30-31). John goes on to emphasize that sentiment above even further, saying that if we say we love God but hate our brother, we are a liar. In other words, love for others and love for God are inextricably tied together in the Kingdom. You can't have one without the other.

People do bad things, act in ways that are often selfish and unkind, and say things that are hateful and mean. Considering that, you may wonder how we are supposed to love others when they are so unlovable. The answer is simple. In our flesh, it is impossible. But we don't have to rely on our own ability to love. We have the benefit of tapping into the supernatural nature of God, who lives in us through the Holy Spirit.

Did you know you can call out God's divine purpose and plan in others? You can—because loving others with God's love is supernatural. His grace is sufficient, no matter the person. Choose today to see others through the eyes of faith instead of fault.

Prayer

"Father, thank you I can fully love others because you first loved me. Thank you for the supernatural ability to see God's design and purpose in every person I encounter. Awaken my heart today to live from your love, not my own weakness, prejudice, or preference. Thank you that as I love others, I can more fully receive your love. I pray, in Jesus' name, amen."

Day 35

I Am Led by the Spirit of God

"For all who are led by the Spirit of God are children of God. So you have not received a spirit that makes you fearful slaves. Instead, you received God's Spirit when he adopted you as his own children. Now we call him, "Abba, Father." For his Spirit joins with our spirit to affirm that we are God's children."

Romans 8:14-16 NLT

It's easy to assume that being led by the Spirit of God is primarily God's responsibility. That somehow, God will supernaturally take over our lives and lead us down the right path. With that mindset, people spend most of their time waiting and hoping something will happen rather than learning to co-labor with God in the process. Hoping year after year for an outcome with no result can cause us to second-guess God's heart and His ultimate plan for our lives. But it doesn't have to be that way.

Being led by the Holy Spirit requires intentionality on our part. We must actively participate in being led. To set the stage for the Holy Spirit's leadership, we must focus our eyes on Jesus, put off the sinful nature by resisting the lure of sin, and purpose in our hearts to live a life that is pleasing to the Lord. It's not about performing for His approval.

In Christ, you are already His beloved and accepted child. As you learn to cooperate with Him moment by moment, you will hear His voice more clearly, recognize His hand at work more quickly, and respond readily in faith. That's what it means to be led by the Spirit.

Prayer

"Father, thank you for adopting me as your child by your grace. I am no longer a fearful slave. I am loved and fully accepted by you. Lead me today by your Holy Spirit. Awaken my heart to know your voice, recognize your leadership and respond in faith all the days of my life. I pray this in Jesus' name, amen."

Day 36

I Have the Mind of Christ

"But the natural man does not receive the things of the Spirit of God, for they are foolishness to him; nor can he know them, because they are spiritually discerned. But he who is spiritual judges all things, yet he himself is rightly judged by no one. For "who has known the mind of the Lord that he may instruct Him?" But we have the mind of Christ."

I Corinthians 2:14-16 NKJV

Have you ever faced a situation where God was leading you in one direction, but it made absolutely no sense to your natural mind? Most believers have experienced this uncomfortable phenomenon and the tension it can often form. It's hard to understand how it will all work out. Thankfully, we're not on our own.

It's the nature of faith and the Christian life to act without understanding everything clearly. Our hope isn't based on what we can see, touch or experience, but is grounded in all that the Lord has promised. It takes intentionality to switch our decision-making to one that's based on God's way of thinking. Thankfully, Paul reminds us that, as believers, we have the mind of Christ and the power of the Holy Spirit within us.

This mind of Christ is available to all those who connect with the Kingdom inside them, and offers every believer unlimited solutions, strategies, and ideas. At any time, you can choose to see, evaluate, and act from God's perspective rather than your own. As you do, your faith will grow and you will mature in your walk with Him.

Prayer

"Father, thank you for giving me the mind of Christ so I can discern the situations of life from your perspective and have access to your unlimited solutions, strategies, and ideas. Awaken my heart today to the present reality—the mind of Christ lives in me. This I pray, in Jesus' name, amen."

Day 37

I Can Do What I See the Father Doing

"Then Jesus answered and said to them, "Most assuredly, I say to you, the Son can do nothing of Himself, but what He sees the Father do; for whatever He does, the Son also does in like manner. For the Father loves the Son, and shows Him all things that He Himself does; and He will show Him greater works than these, that you may marvel."

John 5:19-20 NKJV

Living the Christian life was never designed to be a checklist of dos and don'ts, expectations, or required performance. Unfortunately, what was originally designed as a life-giving relationship with the Living God can quickly turn into dead religion when we don't walk with the Holy Spirit and respond to His leadership. Thankfully, we can trade in the heavy burden of religious responsibility and walk in cooperation with the Holy Spirit in the things He's already doing.

Imagine the everyday freedom that comes from responding to the Holy Spirit's leadership moment by moment - hearing His voice, recognizing His hand at work, then following His lead. That's not some super-spiritual pipedream but what Kingdom living is all about: to do what we see the Father doing. To recognize when He's moving around us. To cooperate with Him by being His hands and feet on the earth.

This is the life Jesus died for you to access and experience. This is the Kingdom that lives inside you. When you follow His lead, God will show up in greater ways than you ever imagined.

Prayer

"Father, I lay down the burden of religious performance before you right now and receive your life-giving leadership in my life afresh. Thank you for including me in your plans to reach others. Awaken my heart to hear your voice and follow your lead. In Jesus' name I pray, amen."

Day 38

I Can Live Free & Refreshed

"Are you tired? Worn out? Burned out on religion? Come to me. Get away with me and you'll recover your life. I'll show you how to take a real rest. Walk with me and work with me—watch how I do it. Learn the unforced rhythms of grace. I won't lay anything heavy or ill-fitting on you. Keep company with me and you'll learn to live freely and lightly."

Matthew 11:28-30 MSG

Sometimes it seems religion has burned out more people than sin ever could. Religion's endless list of expectations, all intended to reach and please God, leaves us feeling inadequate and worthless. The exhausting treadmill of performance, to be more and do more for the Kingdom, even while we feel empty on the inside and spiritually dry, adds unbearable pressure.

No wonder people are leaving organized religion in droves these days. They just can't measure up. Thankfully, God sent His son, Jesus, to die in our place. When we cooperate with the Holy Spirit, He brings us into alignment with Himself so we can easily walk in the benefits and blessings of the Kingdom and enter His rest.

Quit carrying the burden of religious performance around. Lay it down. Because of Christ, you can now live and work from a place of rest, not work for the privilege of experiencing His rest. There's no pressure to perform in the Kingdom, only an invitation to co-labor with Christ.

Prayer

"Father, thank you for sending Jesus to restore me to the fullness of your Kingdom where I can now live life from a place of rest. I am so thankful I get to cooperate with what you are doing in the rhythm of your grace. Awaken my heart to this new reality in Christ and enable me to choose it each day. This I ask, in Jesus' name, amen."

Day 39

I Have Everything I Need with Overflow

"And God will generously provide all you need. Then you will always have everything you need and plenty left over to share with others."

2 Corinthians 9:8 NLT

Depending on how you were raised to think about God and money, you may have a lot of deep-seated beliefs that just aren't true. Religion and people's opinions often skew Kingdom reality. Instead of embracing the idea that we have a loving God of abundant provision, people believe God is stingy, providing only enough for them to barely get by so they don't become greedy. This inaccurate belief about God's heart creates a limiting belief that keeps some from experiencing God's abundant provision.

As God's child, we have been promised His faithful provision. He provides everything we need in this life and more than we could ask for to walk out and accomplish our assignment and be a blessing to those around us. Just because you've not experienced this reality yet, doesn't mean it's not true!

Begin your day by thanking God for His generous and faithful provision. As you renew your mind to this truth, you will find yourself experiencing less anxiety where money is concerned. The Holy Spirit will show you how to receive every good thing the Father has for you. God desires to withhold no good thing from those He loves, both for your benefit and the benefit of those He wants to bless through you. You can trust Him to provide.

Prayer

"Father, thank you for your promise of abundant provision! Thank you, Holy Spirit, for your help, I'm trusting you to teach me how to receive every good thing you have for me. I lay down all limiting beliefs I have held at the feet of Jesus. I want to be all you've called me to be, accomplish what you've called me to accomplish, and be an overflowing pipeline of blessings for those around me. Thank you for being a generous God! In Jesus' name I pray, amen."

Day 40

I Am a Light in the Darkness

"For at one time you were darkness, but now you are light in the Lord. Walk as children of light (for the fruit of light is found in all that is good and right and true) and try to discern what is pleasing to the Lord. Take no part in the unfruitful works of darkness, but instead expose them."

Ephesians 5:8-11 ESV

Before we were saved and restored into the fullness of God's Kingdom, we walked in darkness—operating out of our sin nature. We perceived life through this nature and darkness informed our actions. But now, we have a different reality! We have been transformed from darkness into light.

Our old, sinful nature was crucified with Christ and the darkness in us was eternally destroyed. We have been made alive in Christ—brought out of the fog of darkness into God's Light. Therefore, as children of the light, our very presence reveals the goodness of God.

Every place we go, everyone we encounter can see the transforming light of God we carry.

Instead of trying to figure life out in the dark and on your own, you have access to the Holy Spirit living inside you. And with the Holy Spirit's help, you can discern what is pleasing to the Lord in every situation. But even with your new nature in Christ, you must intentionally choose to walk in the light of His presence. And as you do, your light will dispel the darkness around you. Like the way a flame lights up a dark room, God will shine through you to expose and defeat the enemy's work.

Prayer

"Father, thank you for rescuing me from sin's darkness and making me a light. It delights me to know I carry the light of your presence wherever I go. Thank you for shining your goodness and grace toward every person through me. Awaken my heart to this new reality. I pray this in Jesus' name, amen."

Day 41

I Can Prosper in All Things

"Beloved, I pray that you may prosper in all things and be in health, just as your soul prospers."

3 John 1:2 NKJV

The hustle and grind systems of this world seek to get us to go faster, do more, and produce bigger, better results. Compete, strive, hustle, grind. It's exhausting. Even as believers in Jesus, it's easy to get sucked into a mentality that bases our worth and effectiveness on our performance rather than God's grace. When we cultivate a spirit of striving and performance in our hearts, our thoughts and actions will be forever focused on the never-ending hustle that the world requires.

Thankfully, life in the Kingdom is the opposite of that and wholly different. Kingdom life tells us if we want to be first, then be last. If we want to receive, then give. And if we want our life to prosper on the outside, we must first prosper on the inside. Lasting transformation in the Kingdom happens from the inside out, because whatever we cultivate internally will manifest externally.

As you cultivate a heart of intimacy with the Lord, focus on His promise of rest, provision and protection—your thoughts and actions will then turn toward His purposes for you. You will clearly see the ideas, opportunities, resources, and relationships He has for you. Learn to walk in His rest because prospering externally is the fruit of prospering internally.

Prayer

"Father, thank you that I don't have to participate in the striving race of life the world offers me. Thank you for designing me to live in the reality of your rest, provision, and protection. Awaken my heart today, Holy Spirit, to this new reality so I can prosper internally in all you have for me. It's in Jesus' name I pray, amen."

Day 42

I Have Overcome the World through Christ

"Whoever believes that Jesus is the Christ is born of God, and everyone who loves Him who begot also loves him who is begotten of Him. By this we know that we love the children of God, when we love God and keep His commandments… And His commandments are not burdensome. For whatever is born of God overcomes the world. And this is the victory that has overcome the world— our faith. Who is he who overcomes the world, but he who believes that Jesus is the Son of God?"

1 John 5:1-5 NKJV

The world constantly seeks to convince us that the only way to overcome difficulty and succeed in life is through our own strength. Fake it until you make it. Take charge. Make it happen. These are celebrated virtues in Western culture, yet they have little to do with how the Kingdom of God works. To live life according to the Kingdom requires an intentional mindset shift. A different perspective.

In the passage above, the Apostle John describes the believers' new reality. Belief in Jesus equals new birth and through that new birth, we receive enabling grace. But think of the implications when he says, "*whatever is born of God overcomes the world.*" Ideas and solutions that originate in God and are born of God carry the ability to overcome, defeat, dislodge, and displace the spirit of this age.

As God's child and by His grace, you carry the solutions, ideas, perspectives, and plans to overcome the world. You also carry the ability to release breakthrough in others through co-laboring with Christ by faith. What an opportunity to see His Kingdom come through you!

Prayer

"Father, thank you for Christ's finished work of grace to overcome the world. Thank you that each day I can be a catalyst for breakthrough in the lives of others for your glory. May His Kingdom come on earth, through me! This I pray this in Jesus' name, amen."

Day 43

I Am Safe, Well-Fed, and Restored

"The Lord is my shepherd; I shall not want. He makes me to lie down in green pastures; He leads me beside the still waters. He restores my soul; He leads me in the paths of righteousness for His name's sake."

Psalm 23:1-3 NKJV

As a shepherd, David knew the importance of caring for his sheep. They were his livelihood and under his care. He kept a watchful eye on them, making sure predators had no opportunity to harm them. He led them to the best food, freshest water, and opportunity for rest. In his care, all the sheep had to do was follow his leadership each day. They didn't have to run around trying to find food and water on their own. Over time, they learned to trust their shepherd.

Psalm 100:3, describes us as, *"the sheep of His pasture"* and Jesus himself as our faithful shepherd, carrying for us each day. As we follow our heavenly

Shepherd's leadership, He promises to meet all our needs to the point we are fully satisfied and to lead us into safe places of rest and refreshment, all for our benefit. We don't have to perform to earn it or measure up in any way.

In Christ, you are already His beloved child. Even when you run away and do life on your own for a time and find yourself in a situation that's less than desirable, you can rest in the fact that the Good Shepherd will search for you, find you, and restore you to His care.

Prayer

"Father, thank you for being my Good Shepherd. Thank you for leading me to safe places where my provision is plentiful, and I no longer have to strive on my own. Teach me to live in the reality of your refreshing rest. I choose to follow you today as you lead me. I pray this in Jesus' name, amen."

Day 44

I Am Overtaken by Blessing

"Now it shall come to pass, if you diligently obey the voice of the Lord your God, to observe carefully all His commandments which I command you today, that the Lord your God will set you high above all nations of the earth. And all these blessings shall come upon you and overtake you, because you obey the voice of the Lord your God"

Deuteronomy 28:1-2 NKJV

The children of Israel were given such wonderful promises by the Lord in Deuteronomy 28. Promises to bless them and bring them into all the abundance of His Kingdom. These promises were based on their obedience. If they obeyed His commands, they reaped the benefit of His blessings: their crops and finances, their reputation and relationships, protection from enemies, and their place in the land. Their disobedience brought on a curse.

Thankfully, our new covenant relationship with God is based on the finished work of Jesus. We have been overtaken by the blessings and benefits of His Kingdom. We've been given salvation and eternal life, provision and protection, and the indwelling power of the Holy Spirit to walk in all He's called us to do.

Although God's blessings aren't based on your obedience, they come with a responsibility to walk in the power of the Holy Spirit. You are not to use His grace as an opportunity to sin. Galatians 6:7-8 NKJV is clear, *"Do not be deceived, God is not mocked; for whatever a man sows, that he will also reap. For he who sows to his flesh will of the flesh reap corruption, but he who sows to the Spirit will of the Spirit reap everlasting life."* You can experience all God has for you as you walk according to His Spirit.

Prayer

"Father, thank you for the new covenant and all the blessings that come with it. Thank you that as God's child, I get to walk in all the benefits of Jesus' work. Empower me today, Holy Spirit, to walk worthy as your child, I pray in Jesus' name, amen."

Day 45

I Am Comforted by God's Faithfulness

"When doubts filled my mind, your comfort gave me renewed hope and cheer."

Psalm 94:19 NLT

I've learned over the years that sometimes you just have to shake things up a bit to get moving again. One day as I walked into my art studio on the way to my office, I glanced at a painting I was working on hanging on the wall. Like I often do in the creative process, I took it and turned it upside down to refresh my perspective. As I did, the Lord spoke to me, "Sometimes I turn things upside down in your life so you can see from a different perspective."

If I'm honest, I don't like when that happens. I'm a creature of habit. I like routine and predictability. I'd much rather have steady growth according to an established plan than the excitement of a surprising adventure where everything is always changing. Unfortunately (or fortunately), I don't get to choose. Instead, every day I get the honor of journeying with the Lord, trusting His hand and listening to His voice. In some seasons, His voice is clear and bold, telling me to go here, do this. In others, it's a faint whisper and a deep knowing to stay the course or simply rest in Him.

Regardless of how He speaks and leads, you can trust Him—I know. Even when everything seems like it's turned upside down. Even when your perspective has changed. Even when your view is limited. He is faithful. You can trust Him even when the situations of life seem untrustworthy. And isn't that the point? That through it all, our hope is ultimately in Him as well as the outcome.

Prayer

"Father, thank you that in times of uncertainty, you are faithful. Knowing you are my faithful Father gives me renewed hope and joy. Awaken my heart today to see my life from your perspective and trust you on the adventure. I pray in Jesus' name, amen."

Day 46

I Can Know the Secrets of the Kingdom

"The knowledge of the secrets of the kingdom of God has been given to you..."

Luke 8:10a NIV

Jesus taught the masses through simple parables because it was an easy way to communicate Kingdom truth that was uncomplicated and simple to understand. But to His disciples, He promised the secrets of the Kingdom of God. Imagine having secret intelligence about what was coming into your life before it ever happened. Think about the confidence it would evoke inside your heart. Instead of feeling like you were always catching up, you would have the ability to prepare and be ready for the things coming down the road of life. That's possible when you start listening for God's voice and responding in faith.

God reserves the secrets of His heart for those in intimate relationship with Him. Just like we wouldn't share the intimate details of our life with a stranger or even someone we just met but reserve those details for those we can trust with the deep things of our hearts. The same is true in the Kingdom. As God's child, He longs to share the deep desires and plans of His heart that He has for you.

As you cultivate intimacy with Him through worship, listen for His voice and respond in faithful obedience to the things He is asking of you. Cultivate an atmosphere of trust with the Lord that will yield unending fruit. The secret strategies that He's been keeping just for you and your assignment will light your fire.

Prayer

"Father, thank you for giving me the secrets of your Kingdom as part of my inheritance. Thank you for trusting me with your heart. Awaken me today, Father, to your great love for me. Give me ears to hear your bold declarations and sweet whispers, and a heart to quickly respond. This I pray, in Jesus' name, amen."

Day 47

I Will Not Be Destroyed

"But now, O Jacob, listen to the LORD who created you. O Israel, the one who formed you says, "Do not be afraid, for I have ransomed you. I have called you by name; you are mine. When you go through deep waters, I will be with you. When you go through rivers of difficulty, you will not drown. When you walk through the fire of oppression, you will not be burned up; the flames will not consume you. For I am the LORD, your God, the Holy One of Israel, your Savior."

Isaiah 43:1-3 NLT

It's human nature to avoid difficulty and pain at any cost. Who wants to experience unpleasant things? But it's in those challenging times that we are changed. Walking with God is not a linear path. Life's journey is filled with unexpected twists and turns that often feel like a crooked mountain path. Sometimes we're on an exhilarating adventure with the Lord, while other times, we're lost, confused and frustrated.

Amid painful circumstances, God promises a relationship even though we'd prefer a rescue. Difficult times grow our faith and build our character, soften our hearts and turn us back to the Lord. When faced with seemingly hopeless situations, we learn to trust in His goodness. God's presence is sure. He never leaves us.

You're going to make it. You will not be overcome by the flames or the flood. And even though you might want to be rescued, God promises to walk you through them. No matter what you face, the victory is yours through the empowerment of the Holy Spirit.

Prayer

"Father, thank you that in the middle of circumstances that overwhelm and seek to undermine my faith in you, I have the calm assurance you are with me. I declare today my hope is in you and your power alone. I trust you to grow and mature me in every good and difficult time. Thank you, in Jesus' name, amen."

Day 48

I Have Supernatural Access to Resources

"And I will give you treasures hidden in the darkness— secret riches. I will do this so you may know that I am the LORD, the God of Israel, the one who calls you by name."

Isaiah 45:3 NLT

When pursuing our Kingdom assignment, the enemy's goal is to get our eyes off God's faithfulness and onto our natural circumstances. Especially when it comes to provision. In the natural realm, things like money, relationships, and resources seem limited, only available to a select few. But not so in the Kingdom of God! Not only does God have unlimited resources, He also has the ability to get them to you by any means necessary.

Many ideas and untapped opportunities have remained hidden for generations. God wants to show us how to access these hidden resources so we can fulfill our Kingdom assignments. When we're in alignment with Him and understand our unique design and assignment, Holy Spirit will speak. Through supernatural revelation, He will move us into a position to see, know, and experience things unavailable to others. Why? Because He loves us and wants us to enjoy unhindered Kingdom favor.

When the enemy tries to shift your mind to focus on what you don't yet have, turn your focus to God's promise of supernatural provision. Thank Him for the hidden treasures and secret riches waiting for you in the storehouses of heaven. He wants to give you every good thing you need to thrive in this world. This is His story, and we are a part of seeing it fulfilled on the earth. God, get your glory!

Prayer

"Father, thank you for your faithfulness to provide for my every need in ways that I can't even imagine. I trust that you are positioning me to receive everything I need according to your riches in glory through Christ Jesus. More than I could ask or imagine, in Jesus' name, amen."

Day 49

I Can Love God and Others

"Teacher, which is the most important commandment in the law of Moses?" Jesus replied, "'You must love the Lord your God with all your heart, all your soul, and all your mind.' This is the first and greatest commandment. A second is equally important: 'Love your neighbor as yourself.' The entire law and all the demands of the prophets are based on these two commandments."

Matthew 22:36-40 NLT

In the Kingdom, everything begins and ends with God's love. The Father first loved us and His love enables us to love Him in return. The love that Jesus describes above is an all-encompassing love. A whole-hearted, center of our inner life kind of love where all intention is birthed. A loving with our souls—our will and emotions. With our minds—our reasoning and intellect. Every part of our being must be captivated and informed by the love of God.

The love we have experienced from God must become the prime motivating factor as we interact with others. Jesus calls us to see others through His loving lens: with grace and the Father's perfect intentions, not through our personal preferences and weaknesses.

Purpose in your heart to obey God and love others, remembering how sweet His love felt when you first received it. Your ability to love others will spring up from that deep well. When you offer your wholehearted love to God, the door of the Kingdom will open and begin to flow through you into the lives of others, releasing God's transformative power.

Prayer

"Father, thank you for loving me before I ever thought about loving you. Awaken my heart today to the vastness of your love for me. Help me to love as I have been loved. so that I might be a conduit of your love to others. I pray in Jesus' name, amen."

Day 50

I Am the Temple of the Holy Spirit

"Don't you realize that your body is the temple of the Holy Spirit, who lives in you and was given to you by God? You do not belong to yourself, for God bought you with a high price. So you must honor God with your body."

I Corinthians 6:19-20 NLT

The circumstances of life often tempt us to believe that we are somehow separated from God. The enemy lies to us, saying we are inadequate, disappointing, and condemned. Over time, if those lies take root in our hearts and minds, they produce the fruit of doubt and unbelief, including thoughts, beliefs, and actions that can separate us from God. Thankfully, we can combat those lies with the truth of God's Word.

As believers, we have become the temple of the Holy Spirit. He does not live far off. No! He's living inside of you and me right now. And He's also placed His Kingdom inside of us, giving us full access to all the resources and wisdom we'll ever need. Although our bodies are temporal earthen vessels, we must honor them as a gift from the Lord and as the dwelling place of the Holy Spirit.

Choose today to offer your body as a living sacrifice to the Lord. As you do, God's grace will fill you with all you need to live a life that is pleasing to Him. Though there will be times when you feel out of sync with what you know to be God's best for your life, intentionally care for your body. Nurture it and bring it into submission to the Lordship of Jesus so that, just like in your spiritual life, it honors the Lord.

Prayer

"Father, thank you for the gift of your Holy Spirit, which is living and active in me. Awaken my heart to the reality I now have unhindered access to everything I need through the finished work of Jesus. Help me to honor you by honoring my body and choosing to live a life that is holy, healthy, and worthy of the calling you've given me. I pray this in Jesus' name, amen."

Day 51

I Am United with Christ

"But now you have been united with Christ Jesus. Once you were far away from God, but now you have been brought near to him through the blood of Christ."

Ephesians 2:13 NLT

Almost every child remembers the hurtful feeling of being left out of some childhood game or not being chosen for a team. Waiting for someone to call our name yet fearing that moment would never come. Those experiences often reinforced an already fragile self-image. But the moment our name was finally called, everything changed. Hope and excitement filled our hearts—we were chosen. Everything was going to be ok.

Even though we're far past childhood, most Christians face those same feelings every day because the enemy tells us we are still on the outside looking in. That we are separated from God, unable to access all Jesus restored to us through the cross. But that is a lie —we have not been cut off from the power of new life in Christ.

Don't take the bait. Instead, remind yourself who you are in Christ. You are God's child—redeemed, seated, adopted, sealed, and secure in Christ. A member of the family of God with access, authority, and an inheritance. Seated in Heavenly places in Christ with a supernatural perspective. Able to do all things through Him and receive everything you need from Him. That's who you are!

Prayer

"Father, thank you for bringing me close to you through the blood of Christ. Thank you that even when I was far away from you, you sent Jesus to put me into relationship with you. Remind me today, Lord, who I am in you so I can walk in all that you designed for me before the very foundation of the world. In Jesus name I pray, amen."

Day 52

I Was Created for Such a Time as This

"If you keep quiet at a time like this, deliverance and relief for the Jews will arise from some other place, but you and your relatives will die. Who knows if perhaps you were made queen for just such a time as this?"

Esther 4:14 NLT

Have you ever wondered, considering humanity's monumental problems, if God could use you? Especially when it's so easy to see yourself as small, insignificant, and relegated to your little corner of the world. Your natural abilities are inadequate to solve the problems at hand. How in the world could I ever make a difference, you ask? Thankfully, you're not alone.

Esther was selected, positioned, and given favor at precisely the right time and place in history to accomplish God's will. God loves placing His children in strategic places for significant moments of transformation. Throughout every area of society—at work or at home, among friends or strangers—God is positioning us for Kingdom impact. All we need to do is simply follow His lead and pay attention to what's happening around us.

Just like Esther, you can give God your yes and He can use you in a powerful way to deliver others from destruction. He can place you in situations you never thought possible to bring a supernatural demonstration of His Kingdom to earth, changing people, shifting atmospheres and impacting nations for eternity. Listen today for His voice and obey even when it doesn't make sense. God wants to use you in ways you never dreamed possible.

Prayer

"Father, thank you for your desire to use me to release your Kingdom. Thank you for eyes to see and ears to hear how you lead me. Give me faith to obey you quickly and the grace to walk boldly in circumstances I don't easily understand. Thank you for being faithful to empower my walk with you. I pray this in Jesus' name, amen."

Day 53

I Am Called as a Servant to Others

"Jesus called them together and said, "You know that those who are regarded as rulers of the Gentiles lord it over them, and their high officials exercise authority over them. Not so with you. Instead, whoever wants to become great among you must be your servant, and whoever wants to be first must be slave of all. For even the Son of Man did not come to be served, but to serve, and to give his life as a ransom for many."

Mark 10:42-45 NIV

Jesus' disciples wanted Him to set up an earthly Kingdom, but He had other plans. Just like James and John, we often desire places of influence and power and on our timeline. Using God's principles outside of His presence leads to promoting personal agendas, power struggles and manipulation. Well-meaning people operate out of personal zeal for God rather than co-laboring with Him.

But that's not how God's Kingdom works. His Kingdom is first established in the heart and then naturally overflows into the kingdoms of this world. And one of the primary markers of its establishment is a servant's heart. That's why a change is required. Living in the Kingdom requires daily submission to Christ, being led by His Spirit and serving others.

Our human desires are often in direct conflict with the way God works. If you want to co-labor with God to call for cultural change and foster unity and reconciliation, you'll need His heart full of passion and grace. Submit yourself to the Holy Spirit's leading today.

Prayer

"Father, thank you for the invitation to be a part of establishing your Kingdom on the earth through radical servanthood and the ministry of reconciliation. Awaken my heart to this truth today so I can represent you well, walk worthy of the calling you have given me and accomplish all you have for me in Jesus' name, amen."

Day 54

I Have Overcome the World Through Christ

"You are of God, little children, and have overcome them, because He who is in you is greater than he who is in the world."

I John 4:4 NKJV

The enemy of our soul, Satan, is a very real adversary. The Bible says he comes to steal, kill, and destroy through any means necessary—including distraction and disappointment, discouragement and fear. He sprays fiery darts at our hearts, uses others unknowingly in his scheme and causes general disruption until we simply want to give up. He uses the circumstances of life to weigh us down and wear us out. Thankfully, we have a new reality in Christ.

In the Kingdom of God, we don't overcome by using willpower or some other self-help technique. Victory doesn't come because we beg for help or hope for rescue. It happens because the same power that raised Christ from the dead lives inside of us (Romans 6:10-11).

The power of God is available and active in you! Take hold of God's promise to never leave you or forsake you (Hebrews 13:5-6). Stand and declare the Word of God over your life, no matter what the enemy may throw at you. Decree and declare victory over all that seek to defeat you. Choose to walk in Christ's power today.

Prayer

"Father, thank you for the power of the Holy Spirit, which is living and active in me right now. Thank you that I am an overcomer because you live in me. Awaken my heart to the truth that your Kingdom power lives in me so I can walk boldly as the person you created me to be. Help me remember to declare the Word of God over my life so I can live in victory and you can get your glory. I pray this in the mighty name of Jesus, amen."

Day 55

I Have Been Given Gifts by God

"Do not be deceived, my beloved brethren. Every good gift and every perfect gift is from above, and comes down from the Father of lights, with whom there is no variation or shadow of turning. Of His own will He brought us forth by the word of truth, that we might be a kind of firstfruits of His creatures."

James 1:16-18 NKJV

Deception causes us to believe something is true when it's not. It creates a false reality that, if accepted, becomes our normal. This is an especially effective trick of the enemy when it comes to discerning our unique design in God's Kingdom. He loves to sow doubt and unbelief in our hearts, causing us to question whether our gift or talent is really from God so we never step out into what God placed in our heart. Thankfully, God's Word shines a light on the enemy's lies and reveals the truth.

Since every good and perfect gift comes from the Father, the question is not whether the gift is from

Him but whether we are operating in our gift under the lordship of Jesus and through the leadership of the Holy Spirit. The Kingdom is God's rule and reign over all things. It's all from Him, for Him and operates through Him. Living from a Kingdom perspective allows us to erase the lines between sacred and secular.

Every gift, resource, and opportunity you have has the capacity to be used by God to release His Kingdom on the earth. If you re-orient your perspective to His, He will give you His solutions for every problem you face. Thank God today for your unique design and walk boldly in it.

Prayer

"Father, thank you for designing me with unique Kingdom gifts, talents and graces. Thank you for the invitation to co-labor with you to see your Kingdom come and your will be done on earth as it is in heaven. Awaken my heart today to the reality of your Kingdom living inside me. In Jesus' name I pray, amen."

Day 56

I Am Being Filled with God's Presence

"As the deer longs for streams of water, so I long for you, O God."

Psalm 42:1 NLT

The struggles of life often cause us to feel like we're running a race, out of breath and in need of refreshment. Unfortunately, the enemy uses times like these to convince us God has left us without all we need, alone and on the side of life's road. We desperately long for God to feed and refresh us, begging and seeking God from a place of lack rather than from a place of blessing.

Thankfully, the Word of God tells us that when we seek Him, we will find Him. Our longing for God should always be based on our confidence in Christ, not the desperation we experienced before we knew Him. In Christ, we already have all things and can receive all things by faith. There is no need to beg. He delights in supplying all our needs and fills us until we overflow.

In Christ, you have no need. Through the ministry of the Holy Spirit, you are continually filled and refreshed. You are loved, surrounded and complete in Him—yet He wants to bring you into more ongoing encounters with His love. This is a beautiful Kingdom mystery, a reality you have been invited to live in.

Prayer

"Father, thank you that in Christ, I have everything I need for life and godliness. Thank you that even in times when I feel empty and in need of a refill, you remind me that I am already filled with you. Thank you for inviting me into your refreshing presence, where I am continually filled and renewed. Blow through me afresh today, in Jesus' name, amen."

Day 57

I Am Burning and Building with God

*"The fire on the altar shall be kept burning on it;
it shall not go out. The priest shall burn wood on
it every morning, and he shall arrange the burnt
offering on it and shall burn on it the fat of the
peace offerings."*

Leviticus 6:12 ESV

The cry of the church for generations has been for God
to burn in us, to be that burning bush that Moses saw,
and for Pentecostal flames of fire to dance on our heads.
In the Old Testament, the Levites were responsible for
keeping the fire on the altar burning around the clock.
It was a full-time job. Thankfully, there is no longer a
need for atoning sacrifices because Christ has satisfied
that need once and for all with His death, burial and
resurrection.

Now, the altar is our heart and the sacrifices of
our very lives. We are responsible for keeping our
hearts burning with love for Him. What a wonderful

privilege. For generations, the church has, for the most part, exclusively sought revival. And because of that, we've seen wonderful, yet short-lived awakenings. But there is so much more. Yes, God is looking for those burning with revival fire, but He's also looking for people He can build His Kingdom with for generational and cultural impact.

God wants to use you to advance, build and establish His Kingdom. You are now responsible for keeping the fire burning on the altar of your heart. Stay in His presence, soak in His love, and His fire will steadily burn within you as together you build all He's called you to build with Him.

Prayer

"Father, thank you for the invitation you have given me to burn and build with you. Thank you for your presence that awakens, inspires and motivates me to build with you in the Kingdom. Draw me by your Spirit that I would burn with your glory so others might know you are God. I pray all this in the name of Jesus, amen."

Day 58

I Can Create with the Creator

"In the beginning God created the heavens and the earth."

Genesis 1:1 NLT

Many people see creativity as a special gift for only a select few who are worthy to call themselves artists. They believe their own ability to engage in creativity is deeply inadequate as compared to others and trudge through life without understanding their potential. But creativity is not the exclusive realm of artists like Bach and Beethoven, Michelangelo or DaVinci. Nor is it reserved exclusively for Jesus in the working of miracles. Our Heavenly Father is the Creator of creativity, and we are made in His image.

Creativity is the birthright of every believer and a partnership Kingdom gift. It's how the Kingdom works. And while it carries inherent power on its own, creativity is most powerful when inspired, directed, and filled with Holy Spirit power. Creativity is an invitation to every believer to become a divine portal where God's

Glory and the Kingdom of Heaven intersects with Earth. When we see and agree with Heaven, using our divine design, gifts and graces, we become a conduit of God's transforming power.

When you co-labor with the Holy Spirit, you can see by faith the things that are not yet – and then bring those things into reality. Any idea, hope or desire can be made incarnate. That's how Heaven gets to earth. This co-laboring with God's creativity is available to you right now. See and agree with Heaven, and the Holy Spirit will inspire and lead you in this beautiful process.

Prayer

"Father, thank you for your gift of creativity. Thank you that it's available to me and active in me through the power of your Holy Spirit. Awaken the eyes of my understanding today to see and agree with you. Show me how to see by faith that which exists only in the Spirit so you can use me to bring it into the earth for your glory. I pray this in Jesus' name, amen."

Day 59

I Am Seated with Christ in Heavenly Places

"For he raised us from the dead along with Christ and seated us with him in the heavenly realms because we are united with Christ Jesus. So God can point to us in all future ages as examples of the incredible wealth of his grace and kindness toward us, as shown in all he has done for us who are united with Christ Jesus."

Ephesians 2:6-7 NLT

Imagine, for a moment, being stuck at the bottom of a cold, damp, wet and dark well—the only light shining through an opening at the top, far out of reach. That well would be a place of desperation. Now switch scenes in your mind and imagine you've been hiking on a beautiful mountain trail. Thirsty and tired, you come upon a beautiful well of water. You let down the bucket, draw up fresh water and drink until you are refreshed. In one scenario, the well was a desperate place, but in another, a place of refreshing. What changed? Your position.

Our position changes our perspective and fundamentally alters what we see as real, available and possible. Before we knew Christ, our life was like living at the bottom of the well, desperate and hopeless. Our position was fixed, our efforts futile. But in Christ, we have been given a new position.

You are no longer stuck in a well of desperation because His power now lives in you. Even in times of difficulty, when your earthly position remains the same, you can view life from heaven's perspective and find His power for living. Choose, today, to view life from your new position in Christ.

Prayer

"Father, thank you for rescuing me from the well of desperation and seating me with Christ in heavenly places. Thank you for helping me see things from your perspective, through eyes of faith and possibility rather than doubt and fear. Help me today to reorient my heart and mind to your heavenly perspective. In Jesus name, I pray, amen."

Day 60

I Can Be Filled and Skilled

"Then the LORD said to Moses, "Look, I have specifically chosen Bezalel son of Uri, grandson of Hur, of the tribe of Judah. I have filled him with the Spirit of God, giving him great wisdom, ability, and expertise in all kinds of crafts. He is a master craftsman, expert in working with gold, silver, and bronze. He is skilled in engraving and mounting gemstones and in carving wood. He is a master at every craft!"

Exodus 21:1-5 NLT

God gives us unique gifts (both spiritual and natural) and talents that help us bear His image in the world. These gifts encourage, build up, and bring fulfillment and joy to our lives and the lives of others. Things like music and art are often the first things we think about when someone mentions talents and gifts, but there are other things like business acumen, administration, and compassion. The spiritual gifts listed in 1 Corinthians 12 includes many more.

Bezalel was both filled with the Spirit of God and skilled in his work as an artist. Filled and skilled. That's the Kingdom model for how we mature in our gifts. Otherwise, we are filled with vision but lack the ability to see it come to fruition, or conversely, we rely on our own abilities apart from God's empowering Spirit.

Whether you have been given a spiritual gift like discernment or a natural talent like the ability to sing, draw, run, dance, or speak—all gifts and talents require intentional development and maturity. When you cultivate His presence while simultaneously growing in the skills you need to flourish, your capacity to release God's transforming light and life enlarges.

Prayer

"Father, thank you for filling me with your presence and power. Thank you for empowering me by your Spirit as I develop the skills I need to accomplish all you have for me. Enlarge my capacity to flow with you and become both filled and skilled, I pray in Jesus' name, amen."

Day 61

I Am Empowered to Create Wealth

"But remember the LORD your God, for it is he who gives you the ability to produce wealth, and so confirms his covenant, which he swore to your ancestors, as it is today."

Deuteronomy 8:18 NIV

In Matthew 6:33, Jesus promises that all the practical things we need for our life here on earth will be added to us as we seek first His Kingdom. A powerful promise for all believers right from the mouth of God. But a verse that says God will give us the ability to produce wealth, can lead us to wonder if there's a contradiction. Is He providing what we need or are we creating it?

It's both, and here's why: God's promise to provide is based on our position as His children, not our performance. But God often provides for us THROUGH our unique design—FOR our unique assignment. The Holy Spirit shows us opportunities through what we see, hear, sense, and become aware of. Opportunities that align with our unique design for the purpose of enabling us to accomplish our Kingdom assignment. As we agree with what He's showing and leading us into, provision is created. And as we receive it, our needs are met, enabling us to accomplish our assignment, enjoy the desires of our heart, and be a blessing to those around us.

The more you attune yourself to Holy Spirit's leadership and cooperate with Him, the clearer the provision He has promised you becomes. Regardless of your design, there's no place in society that is "godlier" or "more spiritual" than another. Wherever He has positioned you, there is an opportunity to reveal His life and light through all you do. And wherever He's positioned you, that's where He will provide.

Prayer

"Father, thank you for your promise to provide for me in ways that allow me to co-labor with you in your Kingdom. Awaken my senses to perceive all you are doing so I can create wealth that will enable me to accomplish my assignment, meet my needs, enjoy the desires of my heart, and be a blessing to others, in Jesus' name, amen."

Day 62

I Am Positioned, Prepared, and Prospering

"Joseph's suggestions were well received by Pharaoh and his officials. So Pharaoh asked his officials, "Can we find anyone else like this man so obviously filled with the spirit of God?" Then Pharaoh said to Joseph, "Since God has revealed the meaning of the dreams to you, clearly no one else is as intelligent or wise as you are. You will be in charge of my court, and all my people will take orders from you. Only I, sitting on my throne, will have a rank higher than yours." Pharaoh said to Joseph, "I hereby put you in charge of the entire land of Egypt."

Genesis 41:37-41 NLT

Most of Joseph's life was marked by events not many would desire. The target of his brothers' jealousy, he was left for dead and then sold into slavery. But God had other plans for Joseph. What the enemy meant for evil, God meant for good. He prepared Joseph for leadership through a series of positions that didn't always make sense. And Joseph's faithfulness to God in each situation created an environment for God to promote and prosper him at the right time.

God is still positioning His children today. Even when we can't see the whole picture, He promises to prepare, protect, and prosper us while providing all the wisdom we need for every situation.

As you set your mind on His truth rather than your circumstances, the Holy Spirit will help you see all the God-possibilities and enable you to receive all He has for you. Connect your heart with God's plans and be faithful to obey all He asks. This will create an environment for God to promote and prosper you—all for His glory.

Prayer

"Father, thank you for desiring to prosper me in all my ways as I pursue you with all my heart. Give me eyes to see and ears to hear what you are doing in and around me so I can respond in faith at the right time. I trust your plans for me. I pray this in Jesus' name, amen."

Day 63

I Can See Life from God's Perspective

"When they arrived, Samuel took one look at Eliab and thought, "Surely this is the LORD's anointed!" But the LORD said to Samuel, "Don't judge by his appearance or height, for I have rejected him. The LORD doesn't see things the way you see them. People judge by outward appearance, but the LORD looks at the heart."

1 Samuel 16:6-7 NLT

Things aren't always as they seem. People and situations that seem too good to pass up are often too good to be true. Problems that seem impossible at first are often our biggest opportunities for growth and acceleration. Just like the prophet Samuel in the verse above, we often judge people and situations by outward appearance, which means we act and react in ways that aren't the way God sees things.

Kingdom living requires a change in perspective. One of daily choosing to align your mind with the mind of Christ, to see through His eyes and from His point of view. God sees far beyond our limited view and temporary circumstances. He sees into eternity and invites us to see life through His eternal Kingdom lens. God's perspective enables us to envision possibilities we couldn't imagine otherwise.

Wouldn't you like to solve problems with the Mind of Christ rather than complicating matters with your unrenewed mind? Offer compassion from His heart rather than a judgment based on your own understanding? Facilitate reconciliation rather than being a catalyst for division? Changing your perspective to God's perspective changes what is possible.

Prayer

"Father, thank you that I can see life through your eyes and respond from your love living inside me through the power of the Holy Spirit. Awaken my heart today to hear your voice and respond in faith as one called to release your Kingdom perspective on earth. I pray in Jesus' name, amen."

Day 64

I Am Setting My Mind on a Heavenly Reality

"Since, then, you have been raised with Christ, set your hearts on things above, where Christ is, seated at the right hand of God. Set your minds on things above, not on earthly things. For you died, and your life is now hidden with Christ in God. When Christ, who is your life, appears, then you also will appear with him in glory."

Colossians 3:1-4 NIV

Most people's minds run on autopilot. Our personal experiences, along with our genetic makeup, establish our "normal" status quo. Left unchecked and unchallenged, our "normal" becomes the dominant framework we live by, even though it may, in fact, be very abnormal—especially from a Kingdom perspective. Interpreting life this way separates us from God's goodness and intentions for us. Thankfully, we have a different option.

Colossians 3:1-4 encourages us to set our minds on Kingdom truth, not on the things of earth that clamor for our attention. To experience a new normal, we must put on the mind of Christ and learn to interpret life from a Kingdom perspective. Doing so is one of the greatest privileges and responsibilities we have as believers.

Point your mind in God's direction. Intentionally focus on an outcome that aligns with God's Word. Process your present circumstances and potential through His perspective. When you do, you cooperate with the Holy Spirit in the transformation and renewal of your mind.

Prayer

"Father, thank you for giving me the ability to participate in the transforming of my mind with your Holy Spirit. I choose to direct my thoughts and attention to your Word and your truth. I receive your Heavenly reality as my reality, knowing I am hidden in you. Thank you for giving me the mind of Christ, in Jesus' name, amen."

Day 65

I Can Bless Others as I Prophesy

"Let love be your highest goal! But you should also desire the special abilities the Spirit gives—especially the ability to prophesy... one who prophesies strengthens others, encourages them, and comforts them."

I Corinthians 14:1, 3 NLT

Whether we realize it or not, God is always bringing things to our attention. The more aware we are, the more we will hear God speak. Recently, I was sitting in the waiting room of a local window tinting shop and noticed many unique model cars on display. I asked the Lord if He was showing me something and sensed He was telling me the owner had a special ability to speak into people's uniqueness and unlock people into God's freedom.

After I paid the bill, I took a moment and casually shared this impression with the man. His eyes immediately teared up. He told me that recently God had been turning all his conversations with his clients about "guy stuff" into conversations about the difficulties they were walking through. He shared how he had encouraged one of his clients experiencing significant difficulty in life, and how they both felt God's presence so strongly in that conversation. It was a real confirmation to him and to me that this word I shared was from the Lord.

Prophetic ministry is not just reserved for church meetings or a few select people. Paul said we should all desire to prophesy. We all have the ability to hear God's voice and release it to others. When you do, you strengthen and encourage them in the Lord. The more you practice, the more natural it becomes. Try it!

Prayer

"Father, thank you for giving me special spiritual abilities. Awaken my heart and mind today to sense when you are leading me to share your life and light with others through your gift of prophecy. Give me the boldness to say "yes" to your Spirit nudges and respond in faith, even when I feel nervous about stepping out. I pray in Jesus' name, amen."

Day 66

I Am Overcoming by Taking My Thoughts Captive

"For though we walk in the flesh, we do not war according to the flesh. For the weapons of our warfare are not carnal but mighty in God for pulling down strongholds, casting down arguments and every high thing that exalts itself against the knowledge of God, bringing every thought into captivity to the obedience of Christ."

2 Corinthians 10:3-5 NKJV

As Christ's followers, the difficulties we face often manifest themselves internally before we ever experience them externally. Satan uses thoughts, feelings, fears, doubts, and accusations to tempt and torment God's people. Instead of overcoming through Christ, this can keep God's children in a place of defeat. Thankfully, we can rest assured that is not God's best for us.

As children of God now restored to His Kingdom, we can walk in the new power and authority given to us through Christ. He has provided us with spiritual weapons so we can demolish the strongholds and lies of the enemy. We can rebuke the fear of impending destruction or rejection and our deep feelings of inadequacy by sitting in His presence, tapping into the love of God through the Holy Spirit.

Don't try to fight the enemy with fleshly weapons. Take your thoughts captive and throw them before the feet of Jesus in worship. Allow His presence to wash you with His Word as you replace Satan's lies with God's truth. Soak in God's goodness and allow Him to alter your internal reality. God's weapons are mighty! We no longer have to fight this internal mindset battle alone.

Prayer

"Father, thank you for giving me your power to take my thoughts captive in obedience to Christ. I give you my thoughts, my fears and exchange them for your truth. Teach me to war with your weapons, not my own. Wash me with your presence and set me free from the tormenting fears the enemy throws my way, I pray in Jesus' name, amen."

Day 67

I Am Placing My Hope in God

*"Why am I discouraged? Why is my heart so sad?
I will put my hope in God! I will praise him
again— my Savior and my God!"*

Psalm 43:5 NLT

We all have moments where the volume of our inner life overtakes our focus. Feelings of inadequacy and anxiety cause us to pull back and play small. Feelings like this can cause a flood of emotions and correlating actions that are not in our best interest, much less God's best for our life. Instead of hoping in God and His plans, we expect the worse. Over time, our feelings become an automatic trigger—a learned, practiced, and mastered behavior pattern with a long and successful history of producing results. Just not the ones we want.

Thankfully, we can choose how to respond. We can allow ourselves to go down the slide of our normal automatic response, or we can take a millisecond and ask for Holy Spirit to help us understand why we feel the way we do at any given moment. Today, put your hope in God!

Inviting the Holy Spirit into a moment means you are choosing to hope in God, and teaching your heart and mind to respond to stimuli and emotions in a new, healthy way. You can absolutely retrain yourself to respond in faith, but it takes intention and God's grace working together. Instead of allowing your emotions to rule and produce death, they can become catalysts for healing encounters with God that produce life.

Prayer

"Father, thank you for giving me the ability to co-labor with you in the renewing of my mind so I can become more like you. Remind me to invite you into each moment so I can respond to outside stimuli in a way that glorifies you. Give me faith to choose your thoughts over mine so I can walk in all you have for me as your child. This I pray, in Jesus' name, amen."

Day 68

I Am Walking in Fruitfulness and Multiplication

"So God created human beings in his own image. In the image of God he created them; male and female he created them. Then God blessed them and said, "Be fruitful and multiply. Fill the earth and govern it. Reign over the fish in the sea, the birds in the sky, and all the animals that scurry along the ground."

Genesis 1:27-28 NLT

As stewards of God's Kingdom, God encouraged Adam and Eve to procreate and fill the earth with their offspring, He was also teaching them a spiritual principle. Before multiplication can happen, there must be fruit. It's important we embrace this Kingdom principle as well. God desires each of us to reveal and reflect His image to others so that through us, the world might come to know Him.

What an opportunity we have been given as children of God! Since the dawn of creation, God's original intention for us has been that we would walk in fruitfulness, and it remains His intention today. How do we reflect His image and multiply what He has given us? Through the redeeming, reconciling, and restoring work of Christ.

You have been created in His image and blessed with everything you need on this earth to flourish. Trust God to supernaturally multiply your efforts. Walk faithfully in God's Kingdom and cooperate with Him and the results will be beautiful fruit and that fruit will multiply. No striving needed!

Prayer

"Father, thank you for creating me with intention and purpose; to reveal and reflect your image through my unique design. Thank you for sending Jesus to redeem, reconcile and restore me to your Kingdom. Give me wisdom as I walk with you so my life will produce lasting fruit. As I walk faithfully with you, I know you will multiply my life for your glory in Jesus' name I pray, amen."

Day 69

I Experience Life as I Set My Mind on the Spirit

"For those who live according to the flesh set their minds on the things of the flesh, but those who live according to the Spirit set their minds on the things of the Spirit. For to set the mind on the flesh is death, but to set the mind on the Spirit is life and peace."

Romans 8:5-6 ESV

Our mind can often seem like an uncontrollable minefield of thoughts, feelings and emotions that, when detonated, project chaos onto the screen of our imagination. Thoughts of comparison and inadequacy that produce feelings of condemnation, fear, and shame. Before Christ, we had no ability to change that reality except through our own determination and tenacity. An all too often unsuccessful process.

Thankfully, in Christ, we are new creations with new options. Instead of trying to overcome unhealthy thinking on our own, we can submit our mental processes to the Holy Spirit, who then enables us to see and experience life through the mind of Christ. This empowering grace intentionally directs our mind toward our best life and unimaginable peace.

Create a clear pathway for God in your thoughts and come into agreement with His best for your life. Nurture that new reality internally and it will eventually manifest in your life externally. A beautiful, supernatural process empowered by the Holy Spirit and directed by us.

Prayer

"Father, thank you for the incredible way you created my mind to perceive you, myself, and the world around me. Thank you for enabling me through the power of your Holy Spirit, to bring my mind under your Lordship so I can be inspired and led by you. Give me grace today to set my mind on things of the Spirit and all you have for me so I can be transformed more and more into your likeness. This I pray, in Jesus' name, amen."

Day 70

I Am Walking in New Things in God

"But forget all that - it is nothing compared to what I am going to do. For I am about to do something new. See, I have already begun! Do you not see it? I will make a pathway through the wilderness. I will create rivers in the dry wasteland."

Isaiah 43:18-19 NLT

We've all walked through periods of loss and tragedy, hardship, and pain. Times of testing that felt like they would never end, thinking we missed the boat to the blessings and benefits of the Kingdom. We tell ourselves, we just need to settle for life as it is rather than hope and dream for a brighter tomorrow. But God has something far better for us! He wants to bring new rivers of life to our dry, dead places, along with a new revelation and demonstration of His Kingdom.

New things from the Lord usually come into our life based on how we stewarded what He's already given us. It's a refreshing and renewing of what He's already begun. But we can't receive the new until we've finished what He started in the old. The speed at which God brings new ideas, opportunities, resources, and relationships into our life is often based on how fast we responded to Him the last time He brought one.

Learn to quickly say "yes" to the Lord and respond in faith to the new thing He reveals. If you resist out of fear, unbelief, or stubbornness, you risk spending "40 years in the desert" instead of a two-week trip into the promised land. Acceleration happens as the result of our repeated obedience. He is doing a new thing; don't you see it?

Prayer

"Father, thank you for using every part of my life both for my good and for my growth. Thank you for the new things that are coming. Help me to respond in faith to everything you have for me so I may be found faithful and worthy of the calling you have set before me. Help me steward well all you have entrusted to me, in Jesus' name, amen."

Day 71

I Am Secure in Moments of Transition

"The LORD had said to Abram, "Leave your native country, your relatives, and your father's family, and go to the land that I will show you. I will make you into a great nation. I will bless you and make you famous, and you will be a blessing to others."

Genesis 12:1-2 NLT

Recently I was praying for clarity in my life and business. I felt unsure of myself based on internal feelings and external situations that didn't work out the way I had hoped and planned. Unable to see what was coming in my future, much like Abram, I was in that all too familiar place of transition and tension—between what had been and what was yet to be.

The Father then showed me a picture of a yacht being lifted by a crane and moved from a lake into the ocean. High in the air, awkward, and dripping with water, it was in-between locations as it dangled over the pier. The yacht was being moved to deeper, wider seas so it could run at full capacity.

We are but ships sailed by the master of our hearts. He points and positions us where He will, and our job is to obey. Whether you feel the exhilaration of the wind in your face or the chaffing of the dock, you are His and He is in you. He knows the water you were made for and how to sail you best. Let this knowledge give you the confidence to say yes to all new and uncharted waters.

Prayer

"Father, thank you for your faithfulness to me, especially in moments of insecure transitions. Give me strength to choose your promises over what I see so I can walk in everything you have for me, especially when I'm scared or can't see what's coming, in Jesus' name I pray, amen."

Day 72

I Can See Life through the Lens of Faith

"The hand of the Lord came upon me and brought me out in the Spirit of the Lord, and set me down in the midst of the valley; and it was full of bones. Then He caused me to pass by them all …and indeed they were very dry. And He said to me, "Son of man, can these bones live?" So I answered, "O Lord God, You know." Again He said to me, "Prophesy to these bones, and say to them, 'O dry bones, hear the word of the Lord! Thus says the Lord God to these bones: "Surely I will cause breath to enter into you, and you shall live. I will put sinews on you and bring flesh upon you, cover you with skin and put breath in you; and you shall live. Then you shall know that I am the Lord."

Ezekiel 37:1-6 NKJV

Kingdom living always requires a change in perspective. We view life through one of two lenses: the lens of our experience or our faith. Our experiential lens offers us a viewpoint based on what's possible now by what we've experienced in the past. But God doesn't always make sense in the natural.

To walk by faith, we must set aside the natural to respond to the supernatural. We need to envision possibility through God's power, interpret life through God's Word, see life through His eyes and solve our problems with the Mind of Christ.

Changing your perspective enables you to change your experience and release His transformation. Then, instead of offering others judgment, you can offer them compassion and reconciliation from His heart, and they shall know He is Lord.

Prayer

"Father, thank you for enabling me to see life through your supernatural perspective. Open my eyes, like you did Ezekiel's, to see your plans even when things look hopeless. Give me faith to come into agreement with your supernatural plans in Jesus' name, amen."

Day 73

I Am Rooted & Grounded in God's Love

"I pray that from his glorious, unlimited resources he will empower you with inner strength through his Spirit. Then Christ will make his home in your hearts as you trust in him. Your roots will grow down into God's love and keep you strong. And may you have the power to understand, as all God's people should, how wide, how long, how high, and how deep his love is."

Ephesians 3:16-18 NLT

God's Love is the foundational precept for everything in God's Kingdom. Without His love, life becomes a useless attempt to survive on our own. Because of its preeminence, love is the primary thing the enemy seeks to steal and destroy in us. He knows if he can ground us in something other than God's love, he can ultimately destroy us. God's love must define who we are, or by default, we'll look to others for affirmation, fulfillment, and identity. A mirage rather than life in Christ that produces fruit but not the kind we desire.

As we embrace our connection with Christ, our hearts grow deep roots in His love. This increases our capacity to grow strong in the Lord and accomplish all He's called us to in the Kingdom. We can accomplish infinitely more and experience lasting fulfillment when the love of God is operating in and through us.

Choose today to live from the position of one that is already loved by God rather than performing to earn His love. As you place your roots in Him, you will be empowered and sustained through His unconditional love, no matter the situation or season of life.

Prayer

"Father, thank you for your great love that was poured out for me through your son, Jesus. Thank you for the opportunity to place the roots of my life in your solid foundation. Open my eyes to the ploys of the enemy who seeks my destruction so I may be aware of where my heart is planted. I ask this in Jesus' name, amen."

Day 74

I Am Walking in God's Love Without Fear

"There is no fear in love; but perfect love casts out fear, because fear involves torment. But he who fears has not been made perfect in love. We love Him because He first loved us."

1 John 4:18-19 NKJV

Fear is a tormentor. It tempts us to turn our attention away from an expectation in Christ, toward death and depression, rather than the joyful life every believer has been promised. Fear can attack every area of our life if we let it: from personal reputation, self-esteem, financial provision and anywhere else it can gain traction. It uses our imagination to amplify false narratives and enlarges temptation through seduction, all to get our hearts to come into agreement with its lies. It seems so real in the moment, but fear is a mirage, a false reality that leads to death.

On the cross, Christ defeated fear on our behalf. In Him, we are fully loved and accepted—fully secure.

His perfect love will drive out fear, reveal the enemy's lies, and put on display the futility of Satan's promises. His love reveals who we really are and what's possible, even in the face of an enemy that wants to destroy us. Through His love, life comes into view the way God designed it.

Living from love will enable you to see life's challenges and opportunities through the lens of God's power rather than your own inadequacy. From the perspective of being seated with Christ rather than your own desperation. You can live life with confidence, to be everything and have everything God designed you for without the limitations of fear.

Prayer

"Father, thank you for your powerful love, demonstrated through Jesus, that defeated fear on my behalf once and for all. Awaken my heart so I may walk fearlessly in all you have created me for, in Jesus' mighty name I pray, amen."

Day 75

I Can Receive Wealth from God

"The blessing of the LORD brings wealth, without painful toil for it."

Proverbs 10:22 NIV

Imagine the beauty of the Garden of Eden. Adam and Eve, created in perfection, satisfied and saturated in the goodness of God, had everything they needed to thrive and function in the place God had given them. All the ideas and opportunities, resources, relationships, and authority to do what God put on their hearts to do. And, as the icing on the cake, they walked with God each day in intimate fellowship. That's what I would call ideal. So, what happened?

The enemy attacked God's identity and they believed his lies. Instead of enjoying God's presence and abundant provision, the consequence of their sin cursed their lives and all of humanity. Mankind was forced to toil and sweat to provide for their own needs as they wandered in desperation throughout the earth. Quite a reality shift. Thankfully, everything that was lost through sin's curse has been restored to us by the King through the cross!

Our heavenly Father has given you everything you need for life and godliness, a true gift of grace. Instead of trying to create financial provision on your own, you can receive His abundant blessings by faith. You can live in a place of rest and thankfulness rather than turmoil and desperation. With more than enough (wealth) to embrace your unique design, accomplish your Kingdom assignment, fulfill the desires of your heart and be a conduit of blessing to others.

Prayer

"Father, thank you for restoring me to your Kingdom as your child. Adopted and forever reinstated into the place of blessing, favor, and abundance through your grace. Awaken my heart today, Holy Spirit, that I may receive, by faith, all you have for me. Teach me to walk in Spirit-led expectation and in agreement with your plans and purposes. In Jesus' name, amen."

Day 76

I Am Gifted by God

"For the gifts and the calling of God are irrevocable."

Romans 11:29 NKJV

The gifts God places in us require an intentional process of maturity. Kind of like when people watch a short video clip of a master craftsman creating in their studio and think they could easily create something just as beautiful. But that doesn't mean they could when given the same materials and timeframe. Why? Because the video made the process look easy, but they haven't developed the wisdom and understanding needed to implement such a skill. Knowledge is easy to acquire. It's wisdom and understanding that take time.

God's gifts come to us as seeds, full of potential. We can choose to cultivate the gifts or let them lay dormant. We can also choose how we use them—for our own glory, pleasure and gain—or for the benefit of the Kingdom, in line with our assignment. Some mistakenly think that if we don't use our gifts for

God's Glory, He takes them away. But as the scripture above reminds us, the gifts and the calling of God are irrevocable.

The gifts God gives you belong to you. How you use them is up to you. Investing in your own growth under the leadership of the Holy Spirit honors God. As you offer your gifts and talents to the Lord, it expands your capacity to flow with Holy Spirit inspiration. But you get to choose how to grow and use your gifts. Ask Him to lead you.

Prayer

"Father, thank you for investing your gifts and talents in me. Thank you, that as I embrace my unique design in your Kingdom and cultivate the gifts you've given me, I will see your Holy Spirit move in and through my life. Thank you for the promise of abundant life and the ability to walk in it as I co-labor with you in my gifts, design and assignment. I pray this in Jesus' name, amen."

Day 77

I Have a Delightful Inheritance in the Lord

"LORD, you alone are my portion and my cup; you make my lot secure. The boundary lines have fallen for me in pleasant places; surely I have a delightful inheritance."

Psalm 16:5-6 NIV

In our zeal to do things for God, we often ask the Lord to "expand our borders." To enlarge our capacity to see and accomplish more, not realizing that in doing so, we must remove old borders that were previously in place. As I was praying about this one day, the Lord showed me a cowboy taking down old fences out on the plains. It seemed like removing everything he had worked so hard to build exposed him to potential damage, theft and loss. But I couldn't see the borders God was establishing for him beyond where the old had been, providing greater protection than he'd ever had.

The scripture above reminds us that God has placed our boundary lines in pleasant places. Trusting God, especially in times of transition, often requires a dismantling of the old—good things that have served us well in the last season—along with a willingness to embrace feelings of vulnerability as we step into the new.

Your real challenge in growing isn't a lack of vision, resources or opportunities. It's letting go of what has worked for you before. Let go of the external things that once defined and confined you. Embrace the new and pleasant places Father God has waiting for you. Kingdom expansion is what He is all about and He wants to use you for His glory!

Prayer

"Father, thank you that I have a delightful inheritance in you. Give me grace today to trust your heart for me, rather than my own plans, experience, and comfort. Be my rudder and sail in the open sea. Enlarge my territory and lay my borders in pleasant places. I choose to fix my eyes on you—My God who never fails. I pray this in the mighty name of Jesus, amen."

Day 78

I Know God is Working All Things for My Good

"And we know that all things work together for good to those who love God, to those who are the called according to His purpose."

Romans 8:28 NKJV

No one ever promised us life would be easy. Difficulties and challenges test our willingness to keep going. Tragedy, refinement and seasons of trial cause us great pain. The enemy of our soul loves to use these as opportunities for our destruction. He whispers lies and speaks accusations in an effort to get us to doubt the goodness of God and His purposes for our lives. Accusations that we're not worthy or qualified to stand where God has placed us.

In John 16:33 NKJV, Jesus reminds us *"These things I have spoken to you, that in Me you may have peace. In the world you will have tribulation; but be of good cheer, I have overcome the world."* Because He has overcome the world and the power of the Holy Spirit lives inside us—we, too, have overcome!

As you choose to point your faith toward His conquering ability and away from your own feelings of inadequacy, you can step into the victory He has already accomplished. Instead of believing His lies, remember that God will use life's difficult moments to strengthen and refine you for His Glory. Shape and mold you for His purposes. Reveal the gold He has placed inside you! In the hands of our loving father, every trial and difficulty are opportunities to grow.

My Prayer

"Father, thank you that even as I walk through difficult circumstances, you are faithful to use them for my good and I do not walk through them on my own. Thank you for drawing out the gold you have placed inside me through your refining grace so I can walk worthy of the calling you have given me, not lacking anything. I pray this in Jesus' mighty name, amen."

Day 79

I Can Co-Labor with God to Release His Love

"I tell you the truth, the Son can do nothing by himself. He does only what he sees the Father doing. Whatever the Father does, the Son also does. For the Father loves the Son and shows him everything he is doing. In fact, the Father will show him how to do even greater works than healing this man. Then you will truly be astonished."

John 5:19-20 NLT

When we live under the pressure of religious obligation, the Christian life can seem like an endless list of dos and don'ts. Rules, lists, and expectations that bog down the free flow of the Kingdom living inside us. Instead of freedom and fullness, there's frustration and fear. Thankfully, Jesus came to show us another way to live. The Gospels clearly show us that Jesus operated from Love rather than performed for it. He was both the image and demonstration of God's Love for humanity.

Jesus' life reveals the practical but primary way He connected with the Love of His Father. One we can implement in our own lives. After ministering to the people, He pulled away from the crowds to reconnect and recharge with His Father. Then, as one fully loved, He was free to fully love others. He left the secret place and rejoined the people, where He demonstrated the Father's love to those around Him.

As you pursue God's presence and cultivate His love, you too can love the same as Jesus loved. Fully offering the Father's love to others—becoming a living, breathing demonstration of God's love for all the world to experience.

My Prayer

"Father, thank you for your great love which has been poured out to me through Jesus. Thank you for giving me the opportunity to be a conduit of that love to others as I respond to the movement of your Spirit inside me. Use me Lord and let my life become a powerful intersection point where your love touches and transforms those around me. In Jesus name I pray, amen."

Day 80

I Am Joyful and at Peace in God

"Always be full of joy in the Lord. I say it again—rejoice!... Don't worry about anything; instead, pray about everything. Tell God what you need and thank him for all he has done. Then you will experience God's peace, which exceeds anything we can understand. His peace will guard your hearts and minds as you live in Christ Jesus."

Philippians 4:4-7 NLT

We want that settled, to know that no matter what, we are unconditionally loved and things are going to be ok—we will overcome. But the world trains us early to believe peace comes from external things like job performance, financial stability, notoriety, and other societal standards of success. This performance-based striving is the antithesis of peace. And it won't allow us to rest. We reach one benchmark and then the goalpost magically moves and peace still alludes us. Ultimate success and the peace it promises is a mirage.

The good news is Jesus promised us ultimate peace of mind in John 14:27 when He said, "*My peace I leave with you...*" But it comes in the context of a relationship with the Holy Spirit and His abiding leadership. Through telling God what we need and thanking Him for all He's already done on our behalf.

As you learn to walk with him and cultivate ears to hear, eyes to see and a heart to know, an inner confidence based on that relationship develops. Not because you no longer care about the practical issues of life but because you know that in Christ, you already have everything you need. His peace will supernaturally guard your heart and mind.

My Prayer

"Father, thank you for giving me your gift of perfect peace which exceeds anything I can understand. Thank you that your supernatural peace surrounds me and guards my heart from the lies of the enemy. I choose to walk in your peace today, in Jesus' name I pray, amen."

Day 81

I Am Releasing the Old to Receive God's Best

"It is easier for a camel to go through the eye of a needle than for a rich man to enter the kingdom of God."

Mark 10:25 NKJV

As we mature in the Kingdom, we must pass through a number of "eye of the needle" moments. Designed by God, these moments are an invitation to examine our hearts and our motives—and require a willingness to shed the old to take hold of the new. It's an opportunity to recognize and repent for our reliance on things other than God's voice. For Abraham, it was what was certain and his security. For Paul, it seemed to be his knowledge, authority, and reputation. For the Rich Young Ruler in Mark 10, it was all about what his heart desired and his dependence on wealth.

And it is the same for us today. God divinely crafts these refining moments to help us clearly see if we are choosing our desire, comfort and understanding instead of trusting God in the unknown. Are we willing to voluntarily lay down the things we have drawn strength, identity, and comfort from in exchange for the security of God's presence and what He has promised?

In your "eye of the needle" moments, ask yourself the hard questions. What are the motives of your heart? Are you relying on an internal framework you have built that is replacing your dependency on God? When we lay down the things that so easily entangle us, we are free to pass through, unencumbered, into our next season.

My Prayer

"Father, thank you for inviting me into the good things you have planned for me in your Kingdom. Open my eyes to see all you have prepared for me and trust you along the journey to its fulfillment. Give me grace to persevere in moments when I want to turn back so I can fulfill my unique design and accomplish your assignment for my life, in Jesus' name I pray, amen."

Day 82

I Am Walking Worthy of God's Calling

"Therefore I, a prisoner for serving the Lord, beg you to lead a life worthy of your calling, for you have been called by God. Always be humble and gentle. Be patient with each other, making allowance for each other's faults because of your love. Make every effort to keep yourselves united in the Spirit, binding yourselves together with peace. For there is one body and one Spirit, just as you have been called to one glorious hope for the future."

Ephesians 4:1-4 NLT

Every person that is called by God is entrusted with a part of His nature as an image bearer who reveals and reflects God to the world. Such a high calling and yet, because of the mundane pressures of life, our fleshly reactions often replace purposeful Spirit-led actions. To walk by the Spirit requires spirit-led intentionality.

To lead a life worthy of this calling, Paul encourages believers to pursue five principles. <u>Humility</u>: the willingness to put others first, knowing your identity is in Christ, not in recognition or achievement. <u>Gentleness</u>: the choice to extend kindness and grace in the moments you want to respond harshly. <u>Patience</u>: the willingness to delay gratification in a moment of frustration or desire and to wait in hopeful expectancy as we are empowered by the Holy Spirit. <u>Unity</u>: the choice to prefer and pursue the collective good over our individual desires in honor to one another. <u>Peace</u>: the eagerness to be a conduit of God's abundance, demonstrating our completeness in Him and inviting others into the same.

Choose today to walk worthy of the calling God has set before you.

My Prayer

"Father, thank you for inviting me into your divine adventure and my unique place in it. In moments when I want to react out of my old nature, give me grace to respond by the Spirit so I can walk worthy of the calling you have set before me as your child. This I pray in Jesus' name, amen."

Day 83

I Am Confident in My Identity, Design & Assignment

"When He had been baptized, Jesus came up immediately from the water; and behold, the heavens were opened to Him, and He saw the Spirit of God descending like a dove and alighting upon Him. And suddenly a voice came from heaven, saying, "This is My beloved Son, in whom I am well pleased."

Matthew 3:16-17 NKJV

Striving is something that comes naturally to most people. It's the normal operating procedure of the world. The fruit of walking under sin's curse since the fall of humanity in the Garden. Sin resulted in our separation from God and a reliance on our own abilities—producing independent desperation. But in the Kingdom, there's a better way. Instead of finding our identity in what we do, we realize our assignment is based on who we are in Christ.

Lasting transformation in the Kingdom always happens from the inside out. As our identity is established in Christ, our unique design is uncovered, and our Kingdom assignment is revealed. Over time, as we cooperate with the Spirit's leadership, God faithfully brings us into maturity— fulfillment and joy through alignment and refinement.

Pursuing your design from a healthy identity in Christ leads to the benefits and blessings of the Kingdom. As you embrace your unique design and Kingdom assignment with gratitude, obedience, and the faithfulness of a son or daughter—God's grace, impact, and provision will shine forth.

My Prayer

"Father, thank you for the transforming power of your Holy Spirit which lives in me. Help me today to live from the inside out as I remember who I am in you, honor my unique design and walk in the Kingdom assignment you have given me. I pray this in Jesus' name, amen."

Day 84

I Am Confident in God's Promises

"For all of God's promises have been fulfilled in Christ with a resounding "Yes!" And through Christ, our "Amen" (which means "Yes") ascends to God for his glory. It is God who enables us, along with you, to stand firm for Christ. He has commissioned us, and he has identified us as his own by placing the Holy Spirit in our hearts as the first installment that guarantees everything he has promised us."

2 Corinthians 1:20-22 NLT

Christians who aren't experiencing fulfillment and joy in their walk with Jesus often complicate Kingdom living through religious pursuits. The simplicity that Jesus offers us is replaced with more "spiritual" activities. I've met so many believers over the years who are completely exhausted because they are focused on things like praying for revival, spiritual warfare, social injustices, and political issues of the day. They pursue these "good" things out of personal zeal and obligation without the grace needed to do it. It's easier for the religious mind to focus on things that "seem spiritual" rather than the simplicity of living in the freedom and power the Kingdom of God offers every believer.

Walking in the fullness of who God created us to be places Jesus on the throne and glorifies His name. This IS the spiritual warfare that causes demons to flee. Passionate prayer—co-laboring with the Holy Spirit— becomes a catalyst for a move of God in our world.

Don't just pray for others aimlessly, pray confidently in the power and promise that is yours through Christ. Pray with a heart to see God move, to do all the wonderful things you've been asking to see happen.

My Prayer

"Father, thank you that your promises toward me are yes and amen. Thank you for adopting me as your own and inviting me into your incredible, eternal Kingdom. Help me to walk in the fullness of your intention for my life so I can glorify you, I pray in Jesus' name, amen."

Day 85

I Am Able to Do All Things with God

"But Jesus looked at them and said to them, "With men this is impossible, but with God all things are possible."

Matthew 19:26 NKJV

When we see life and all its possibilities through the eyes of our own strength, we are often left feeling inadequate and defeated. Right where the enemy wants us to be: completely separated from the miracle-working power of Christ that lives in us. Imagine Jesus seeing us whom He died to restore, choosing to walk in our own strength, struggling every day when we've been given all things. Imagine the Holy Spirit waiting to guide us on an ultimate divine adventure and God's children not realizing a Spirit-led adventure is even an option. It keeps us powerless, ineffective, and frustrated. Definitely not God's ideal.

The enemy doesn't have to tempt us with overt sin to defeat us. He simply has to convince us we're not good enough, smart enough, qualified, healed, or spiritual enough to step into God's glorious plan. If he can do that, he's made a major step toward defeating us. Everything we do will be based on proving our worth and ability to ourselves, God and others, or hiding because of our deep feelings of inadequacy. Not living in the assurance that we're God's beloved children.

Thankfully, in Christ, all things are possible when we believe. Through faith, you can accomplish everything God has designed for you. Instead of focusing on your perceived inability, set your heart in agreement with the power of Christ living in you. Believe and walk in His power today.

My Prayer

"Father, thank you for your Holy Spirit power that lives in me. Thank you for the gift of faith, which enables me to believe that all you have said about me and for me is true. Thank you that Christ has made me good enough and qualified enough to step into Your glorious plan. Awaken my heart to this new reality today so I can experience abundant life. In Jesus' name I pray, amen."

Day 86

I Am Free from Sin

"There is therefore now no condemnation to those who are in Christ Jesus, who do not walk according to the flesh, but according to the Spirit. For the law of the Spirit of life in Christ Jesus has made me free from the law of sin and death"

Romans 8:1-2 NKJV

Sin's promise tempts us with a vision of life as it could be when we follow our own desires apart from God's will—a false reality, a mirage and a fading mist. Thankfully when we come to Christ, we are freed from sin's curse and punishment; but most of the time the enemy doesn't stop his assault. He just changes his tactics to include ruminating thoughts, haunting memories, and condemnation—convincing us we are still unqualified because of whom we used to be prior to our salvation.

Thankfully in Christ, we are new creations. The old has gone, and the new has come. Our sins have been forgiven and cast into the sea of forgetfulness. And when the Father sees us, He sees Christ in us. What a gift! But it's our responsibility to remind ourselves of this Kingdom reality each day so that the gift of Christ can permeate every part of our being.

Remind yourself who you are and cooperate with the Holy Spirit in the renewing of your mind. Take captive the condemning lies of the enemy. Cast them off and replace them with the truth of God's Word. As you do, the framework of your inner life and the lens through which you see yourself will come into alignment with the truth of God's Kingdom, and you'll walk out of sin's condemnation into greater freedom in Christ.

My Prayer

"Father, thank you for your glorious gift of freedom in Christ. Thank you for setting me free from the law of sin and death, and all the condemnation that comes with it. Awaken my heart today to this truth so I can walk in your freedom. In Jesus' name, I pray, amen."

Day 87

I Am Confident God is Directing My Steps

"A man's heart plans his way, but the Lord directs his steps."

Proverbs 16:9 NKJV

Wouldn't it be nice if we could each receive a personal letter or text message detailing the intricate plans the Lord has for us for the next 25 years? Of course it would, but that's not how the Kingdom of God works. Probably because God knows that we would run ahead and try to accomplish everything in our own strength and for our own glory. Discovering God's plan is more like finding and fitting the pieces of a puzzle together than having a golden scroll of revelation float down from heaven.

That's the adventure. And that's why His plans must first be based in our identity in Christ. Without this foundation, we will end up pursuing things that have nothing to do with our design or assignment. And when that happens, there's no peace, provision, opportunity, or favor. The scripture above reminds us that it's our responsibility as God's children to dream with Him. And as we do, we can trust that He will direct our steps. Why? Because all those things freely flow when we walk in alignment with how God created us.

God's plan is not something He is going to force on you. It's something He'll uncover as you involve the Holy Spirit in the discovery process. God plants the seed of inspiration, and you respond in faith. And as you start to plan and pursue the things of God, you can trust that He will direct your steps. But it is your responsibility to initiate the planning process with Him. Remember, as you step out, God shows up.

My Prayer

"Father, thank you for your promise to direct my steps. Thank you for the opportunity to co-labor with you in seeing your Kingdom established on the earth and your presence transform this world. Awaken my perception today so I can come into agreement with your purposes and plans for me. I pray this in Jesus' name, amen."

Day 88

I Am Strengthened in the Lord

"For thus says the Lord God, the Holy One of Israel: 'In returning and rest you shall be saved; In quietness and confidence shall be your strength.'"

Isaiah 30:15 NKJV

When life doesn't go the way we plan, our natural tendency as humans is to struggle and strive to get things back on track. Anger and frustration build up inside. We compare our experiences to those around us and evaluate the next steps by what seems to make sense in our natural mind. Emotionally driven reactions replace prayerful steps of faith. While these may be our automatic responses as humans, it's not the ideal way God designed us to live life in His Kingdom.

We can't strive or scream and complain until we make something happen. No. In the Kingdom, there's a different way—opposite from the way the world works. If you want to be first, then be last. If you want to be a great leader, then be a servant to the least among you. If you want to receive, then give. The same is true with how strength comes to us as God's children.

Just like you rested in the saving power of Jesus for your salvation, you must also return and rest in Him daily for your nourishment and preservation. When you do, a quiet, confident trust will develop in your life, proof of your trust in God. As the world goes crazy around you, your faith in God will be your strength. Return to the Father when weary, He promises to give you the rest you are looking for.

My Prayer

"Father, thank you for your promise to care for and strengthen me. I trust your heart for me; every day you uphold and protect me, regardless of what goes on around me. Give me faith to stand in quiet confidence and draw strength from you so I may glorify you in all things. This I pray in Jesus' name, amen."

Day 89

I Am Satisfied and Blessed in God's Presence

"For a day in Your courts is better than a thousand. I would rather be a doorkeeper in the house of my God than dwell in the tents of wickedness. For the Lord God is a sun and shield; The Lord will give grace and glory; no good thing will He withhold from those who walk uprightly."

Psalm 84:10-11 NKJV

Many believers grow up thinking that God is a hard taskmaster who doles out meager blessings, barely providing for His children for the purpose of making them more spiritual. Their lack is somehow a test or a way to prove they are someone God can use. What a huge difference from what the Bible actually teaches about our generous Heavenly Father.

From the beginning of time, God's heart has been to pour out blessings and favor upon His children. To equip us for every divine assignment He has called us to—to make us a blessing to others while fulfilling the desires of our hearts. Jesus came that we might have a full, abundant life in every area: spiritually, relationally, creatively, financially and in every realm of life.

You have been blessed with everything you need so you can reflect the beautiful nature of our Heavenly Father here on earth. The only caveat is that you walk with Him. God will withhold no good thing from you when your heart is completely His. He wants you to enjoy life in His presence while reflecting His image and nature to those you encounter. To walk boldly as His child with everything you need to accomplish every dream He puts in your heart.

My Prayer

"Father, thank you for wanting to bless me, your child. Forgive me when I've believed you weren't as good as you really are. Awaken my heart today to your generous desire to pour out everything I need for this Kingdom life. I pray this in the mighty name of Jesus, amen."

Day 90

I Am Comforted and Protected in God's Presence

"Yea, though I walk through the valley of the shadow of death, I will fear no evil; for You are with me; your rod and Your staff, they comfort me. You prepare a table before me in the presence of my enemies; you anoint my head with oil; my cup runs over. Surely goodness and mercy shall follow me all the days of my life; and I will dwell in the house of the Lord forever."

Psalm 23:4-6 NKJV

Jesus said that in this world, we would all have trouble. And how true that is, even when we are trying our very best to live according to God's plan. We often watch adventurous movies and like to imagine ourselves courageously facing down our enemy, but all too often, our reality is far from that—mired in mediocrity and not very victorious. Instead of feeling like the overcoming hero, we can feel like the flailing victim.

But God's Word is an anchor in the storms of life, a shield against the fiery darts of the enemy. His truth extinguishes the enemy's attacks and brings all his lies into the light. Life is full of opportunities to choose God's truth over the enemy's mirage. Choosing to walk through hard places by faith—that is where our character is developed and victorious faith is born.

As you declare God's promises in moments of fear, His light will shine forth and His goodness will be displayed in front of the very one trying to destroy you. In the peace of His presence, you will learn to boldly walk through difficulties with new authority. Goodness and mercy really will follow you when you learn to stand on Kingdom truth. That's our God! That's His promise.

My Prayer

"Father, thank you for covering me with your presence and strengthening me with your love so that I may endure difficulties rather than trying to escape them. Help me to trust you in these moments, knowing that difficulty produces character and endurance as I stand firm on your word. I ask this in Jesus' name, amen."

Final Thoughts

I trust our heavenly Father spoke to your heart as you sat with Him and meditated on these Kingdom truths for 90 days. I pray a Kingdom framework has been built and established in your heart as you've invested this quality time with Him. That you now know better who you are and much more about your unique Kingdom design and assignment. He has good things planned for you.

Remember, the Kingdom of God is eternal and all-encompassing. It is like a mighty, rushing river that is flowing with the grace, power, provision, light and life of God. Jesus promised this river would flow through us. When you come into agreement with the Kingdom of God, you flow with its grace, power, provision, life and light. Your design is awakened as you resonate with God's nature. Your assignment feels effortless and natural.

This feeling of momentum is not because you're doing everything right or because there are no challenges but because you're flowing with the river of God's Kingdom. You can't help but thrive. And in difficulty, you remain surrounded and buoyed by the Kingdom's all-encompassing grace. The Kingdom is everything - the new reality Jesus invites us into as His restored children - containing everything we need to live, grow and thrive for all eternity.

If you would like to continue the work you've begun here, consider getting a copy of my book, *God's Plan for Living: A Simple Roadmap to Your IDEAL Kingdom Life*. I know it will be a blessing as you continue to grow and mature in the Lord. I love you, my friend, and I'll see you on the journey.

About the Author

Matt Tommey is an author, artist, entrepreneur, and mentor who is passionate about helping people live in the abundance of God's Kingdom. Through his personal growth journey and extensive work mentoring artists, Matt learned how to make Kingdom principles easy to understand and apply to everyday life so anyone can experience abundant life in Christ.

He currently lives in East Texas with his wife, Tanya, and their son, Cameron, where he enjoys life with friends and family, gardening, and creating original artworks.

Since 2009, Matt has primarily mentored artists who want to thrive spiritually, artistically and in business. He is a successful entrepreneur, popular conference speaker, podcast host (The Thriving Christian Artist), author of 7 books for Kingdom creatives and is recognized internationally as a leader in creativity and the arts. Through his new book, God's Plan for Living, Matt is taking the Kingdom principles he's learned in mentoring artists and sharing them with the world.

To find out more about Matt and the work he does, please visit http://www.MattTommeyMentoring.com.

Printed in Great Britain
by Amazon

26156790R00110

DAILY ENCOURAGEMENT FOR KINGDOM LIVING

Discover the transformative power of the eternal Kingdom of G
"*Awakening to God's Kingdom Within*." In this captivating devotiona
Matt Tommey draws from the principles of his bestselling book, "*God's
Living*," to provide practical and uplifting guidance for daily living.

Immerse yourself in the unstoppable current of God's grace, power, p
light, and life as you align your heart with the Kingdom's divine flow in
Experience the effortless synergy between your true design and God'
allowing your purpose to unfold naturally.

Each day, "*Awakening to God's Kingdom Within*" offers a faith-
affirmation, scripture verse, devotional reflection, and heartfelt prayer
crafted to draw you closer to the Lord. Embrace God's IDEAL for you
uncover the abundant blessings He has prepared for you.

With its timeless wisdom and encouraging words, this devotional wil
your faithful companion, a source of constant inspiration, and a guide to
walk confidently into the fullness of all God has in store for you. Let "*A
to God's Kingdom Within*" uplift and empower you on your spiritual jou

Matt Tommey is an author, artist, entrepreneur, an
who is passionate about helping people live in the a
of God's Kingdom. Through his personal growth jou
extensive work mentoring artists, Matt learned hov
Kingdom principles easy to understand and apply to
life so anyone can experience abundant life in C
currently lives in East Texas with his wife, Tanya,
son, Cameron, where he enjoys friends and family, g
and creating art.